WHERE IS MY CHILD?

Where Is My Child?

MEG SCOTT

KINGSWAY PUBLICATIONS
EASTBOURNE

Unless otherwise indicated, biblical quotations are from the
Holy Bible: New International Version, copyright © International
Bible Society, 1973, 1978, 1984.

Cover design by Drummond Chapman

*Although this is a true story, all names
and physical descriptions have been changed
to protect the identity of those mentioned.*

Printed in Great Britain for
KINGSWAY PUBLICATIONS LTD
Lottbridge Drove, Eastbourne, E. Sussex BN23 6NT by
Cox & Wyman Ltd, Reading.
Typeset by CST, Eastbourne.

Contents

Foreword

A recent BBC radio broadcast involved one hundred 18–22 year-olds handpicked for social class, occupation, sex, and ethnic background.

'The Radio 4 Generation' revealed that all but one of these young people were employed. In sexual matters the AIDS scare was having little effect on their behaviour. One of the group admitted to being a virgin and one to being homosexual. Three could have been described as racists.

As I write this foreword twenty-five people in my home town have been arrested on various offences for drug-pushing. Two young people called at my house very distressed that one of their friends had been found with £1,000 worth of drugs in her house. Would I take a Bible to her in the cells?

In my experience as a pastor this is the real world where Christian families are increasingly struggling to survive. Often they have to contend with the in-experience of church leaders ill-qualified to advise on drug abuse. Parents wrestle with personal guilt and remorse that they are responsible for their children's plight. Home life becomes unbearable as other members of the family feel threatened by the insecurity of the trauma.

Spiritually there is a high price to pay as faith wrestles with the ancient dilemma of God's apparent abandonment of people he is meant to be caring for.

If you have read this far you will realize I am commending this particular book to you. Meg Scott and her family are personal friends and I have used her skills as a caring counsellor on many occasions with people in distress. The ministry which God has given to her comes across on the printed page.

Surely you will identify with a mother's anguish seeing her child destroyed by drug-abuse. Sit with her in the psychiatrist's surgery suffering humiliation. Go with her to the police station in the middle of the night. Attend court with her and hear the charges read out and feel the indifference of the daughter. Stand with her in the squalid conditions of a bed-sit which is home for her child. Feel that sense of being locked into a situation over which you have no control, simply waiting for your child to create the next crisis.

Some of the most moving passages in this book are the conversations between mother and daughter. You may be tempted to be critical and feel you would have handled each situation in a different way. I guarantee you will benefit by the way Meg sought to live out the promise that God gave her for her three children.

If you are seeking to find a place of peace in an unresolved ongoing story, this is the book for you.

DAVID COFFEY

Preface

It was the persuasiveness of a friend which first launched me into authorship in 1979. I had written a letter to her, and she insisted that I should send it to a Christian newspaper. I did, and it was published. It was at this point that I fully realized the power of the written word.

The letter had contained little more than a moan regarding my status as a Christian divorcee: ordinary words describing extraordinary events (though less so in these days), and what I believed were my own personal feelings and reactions. I found it humbling in the extreme that those ordinary words could evoke such a response from others. For what I had believed to be extraordinary events and my own personal feelings turned out, in fact, to be shared by many. Almost all without exception, prior to reading my letter, had felt alone and cut off—both by the 'stigma' of their circumstances and by the guilt which their reactions had aroused in them.

The Tug of Two Loves and *Divorced but Not Defeated* (Torbay Publishing Ltd) came into being as a result of my discovery. In sharing more deeply the story of conflict between my love for an unsaved husband and Jesus, my new-found love, and the ultimate demise of my marriage, I have learned more of that isolation felt by others in similar circumstances. And still it both amazes and humbles me that they are helped by what I have written.

Yet is it really so amazing? Is not the whole mystery of the Bible the fact that ordinary words telling the stories of ordinary people can be breathed into life by the power of the Holy Spirit in such a way as to touch the lives of its readers? It is in identifying with another—his problems, and the solution to those problems—that I may find help myself. But sharing carries with it a degree of vulnerability. One is always open to criticism, the more so when the story involves the lives of others, especially those whom one loves. Feelings of betrayal are inevitable. Yet can I keep silent about what God has done? More to the point, would my silence prevent others from knowing his goodness and experiencing for themselves what he longs to do in their lives?

The story contained within these pages is essentially *my* story: the story of a mother's anguish as she watches the child she has brought into the world going her own way and systematically destroying her life through drug abuse. Sadly, something akin to the circumstances described will already be the experience of many caring parents, but for them, as for me, there is hope and the certainty of another Parent whose love and wisdom never fails.

Of Vicky's story, other than as I have perceived it, I have no knowledge. Those who have lived similar lives themselves will no doubt be better able than I to stand in her shoes, to understand her cravings, to know her despair. And for them, as for her, there is hope. For this is also the story of God's own anguish. Brooding over his fallen world as a mother over her child, he watches sadly as we choose to ignore, spurn and reject the precious gift of life in his Son Jesus. Yet even as we seek those dubious pleasures which will ultimately destroy us—for ever—he is ever-present, ever-loving, desiring only that we should turn to him.

For all who read these pages, I join with Paul in saying: 'I want you to know how much I am struggling for you . . . and for all who have not met me personally. My purpose [in writing this book] is that they may be encouraged in heart and united in love, so that they may have the full riches of complete understanding, in order that they may know the mystery of God, namely, Christ, in whom are hidden all the treasures of wisdom and knowledge' (Colossians 2:1–3).

MEG SCOTT

I

At the End of a Needle

The telephone bell was shrill and clamorous, an unexpected intrusion since it was close to midnight. It
startled me, causing me to jump, so that some of my tea
slopped into the saucer. Carefully putting it on the bedside cabinet, I picked up the receiver.

'Hello? Mum?'

The voice was that of my middle daughter, Victoria.
An image of her round face, green eyes and fair, wavy
hair arose in my mind, while the cold hand of fear
clutched at me. Whatever had happened to cause her to
ring out of the blue so late at night? It was months since
we'd heard from her.

'Vicky! What a lovely surprise . . . .'

'I can't come home for Christmas, Mum,' she interrupted.

My heart pounded. Take it easy, now. This was to be
her first Christmas home for two or three years. One
wrong word from me, I knew, could wreck all such
prospects. The relationship between us was so tenuous:
a fragile, slender hope—no more.

'Is it the train-fare, love? I could send something if
that's the problem.'

She began to cry. 'No, it's not that. I don't know how
to tell you.'

'Vicky, what is it?' Now I was really alarmed. Caution was thrown to the wind.

'I'm on heroin, Mum.' The tears had stopped and her voice came cold and flat down the phone.

The shock must have registered on my face because my husband, Peter, looked enquiringly at me from the other side of the bed. How would he feel about this? He wasn't even her father, and we'd been married for so short a time. I ran my fingers anxiously through my dark curls.

'Oh, Vicky.' The words were expelled on a long-held breath.

'I'm mainlining,' she continued. Then obviously sensing that the jargon was outside my sphere of knowledge and understanding, and in response to my feeble noise of enquiry, she explained. 'Injecting into my veins,' she said, still in the same flat tone of voice.

I felt sick, and had to swallow hard against the rising gorge.

'How . . . how long?' It was like talking to a stranger. This was the sort of thing that happened to other people, the sort of thing one read about in newspapers. It didn't happen to you; to the families of decent, law-abiding citizens; to children who were loved and wanted.

'Two years,' she said, and now, at last, her voice broke once more. 'Oh Mum! I'm so frightened. I want to stop. I need help. I want so much to be with you all. It was awful last Christmas, knowing you were all together. I wanted to be with the family, but couldn't.'

'Darling, we'll help.' My hand shook as I gripped the receiver tightly.

'Could I come down, anyway, Mum? Please?'

'Of course you can. We'll work something out.'

'You won't tell anyone, will you? Promise? I don't want Gran and Gramps to know, nor Aunty Pat and Aunty Sally.

'I'm going to see a doctor up here in the New Year.' Her voice had grown stronger as she detected some sense of hope. 'I could probably get enough stuff to last me a few days over Christmas. And I wouldn't inject.'

'Vicky, I'll have to tell Gran and Gramps. I can't take you into their home without their knowing the situation. I couldn't deceive them like that—it wouldn't be fair.'

'Oh, Mum, they won't have me if they know.' Vicky's voice broke.

'I think they will,' my own voice strengthened. All my life my parents had risen to any and every occasion, and though I knew they would be as grief-stricken and anxious as I was, there was no shadow of doubt in my mind as to what their response would be. 'But we must give them the opportunity to choose for themselves, Vicky.'

'OK,' she agreed reluctantly. 'But not the rest of the family. And, Mum, would you have a word with Dr Engles to see if he can get me anything to help? You can get methadone from the health service to help you get off heroin.'

I promised to make enquiries as soon as possible the next morning; then we said our goodbyes, and rang off. Awareness of my surroundings crept once more into my conscious mind. The night air struck cold on my shoulders, and turning towards Peter, I shivered involuntarily. For a moment I said nothing. Then, in a sudden rush, the pent-up emotion was released in a flood of tears as Peter held me in his arms.

All through the long night sleep eluded me as I lay thinking and praying. From time to time snatches of the past unfurled before me, like clips from a cine film: scenes of Vicky's childhood, the joys and tragedies of her twenty years of life, or at least such as were known to me. Thinking back to the tiny form that had come into the world all those years before, it seemed such a waste. And could I hold myself blameless? I knew I could not.

It was with a sick heart, drained and exhausted, that I saw Peter and Ruth, my youngest daughter, off next morning. If she noticed anything as she prepared to leave for school, she made no comment, and sensitive to her own emotional problems, we made no reference to Vicky's phone call.

'Only two more days at school,' Ruth said, excitedly. 'And only a week to Christmas. I must wrap my presents tonight. Can you get me some more paper, please, Mummy?'

Smiling wanly, I listened to her chatter, then turned wearily back into the house, shutting the front door behind them. A terrible thought had come to me during my enforced reminiscences of the previous night, and I wanted to check whether it had any foundation. Picking up the phone, I sat on the bottom step of the stairs, still in my night-clothes, and dialled the number of one of the elders at our church.

'Gerald, it's Meggie here,' I began as soon as the connection had been made. Without further preamble, I launched straight in, urgently requesting some reassurance. 'Do you think it's possible to reject a child in the womb? I mean, if you don't want the pregnancy, can the unborn child pick up a sense of being spurned, and could that affect the child throughout her life?

It had been during my prayers of the night before that the idea had first manifested itself. If it had come from the Lord, then it was obviously an area that needed to be dealt with; if not, then the Enemy was trying to tie me up in a false sense of condemnation. Either way, I had to know. For it had become apparent to me, with a sudden and startling clarity, that Vicky's situation had not come upon her in recent years, nor had it been unheralded. Throughout her life, right from the word go, she'd been different—different and difficult.

Was it possible, I wondered, to trace her drug dependency back to some character flaw, or some circumstance pertaining at the time of her birth or conception? Is it possible for parents to recognize early in childhood the potential areas of risk to their offspring in later life? More to the point, can anything be done to avoid such deviant behaviour, to steer our children in a different direction, to bring about such changes of character as are necessary for the child's healthy development? And even when, like me, the whole question is in retrospect, can anything be done to arrest the downward spiral and to effect a healing in your child?

These were the questions that plagued me on that December morning, and formed the start of a quest for knowledge and understanding of just how big and how powerful and how loving was the God whom I worship, especially in the area of trusting him with my loved ones. More particularly, was he able to reach into the mind of a drug addict, crazed, distorted and dulled by the effects of heroin? Could I really have confidence in his love for my daughter?

The key, I was sure, lay in those long-forgotten scenes from years before which had flashed up in my memory during the night. It all began with Vicky's birth—and all that had led up to it. It was strange really, though I hadn't realized it at the time—even her mode and manner of entering the world was quite different from the birth of my other two daughters. Where they seemed to have a sleepy reluctance to leave the security of the womb, Vicky, it seemed, could hardly wait to do things in an ordered manner. She so nearly caught us all out.

PART 1

The Stealthy Intruder

2

Daddy's Darling

It was late evening, twenty years earlier, when without warning my waters broke, heralding Vicky's rushed entry into the world. With Sarah's birth already behind me, and that having been so easy, I felt calm. So much so, that I ended up having to make tea for the rest of the family, all of whom had been thrown into utter panic by the speed of events!

We'd had a mother's help, a young country girl, who'd actually proved more of a hindrance, and when she had stubbed her toe a few days earlier, with disastrous results, I'd willingly sent her home.

'I'm afraid Debbie's going to have to rest with her foot up for at least a week,' the doctor had said. 'The toe-nail is septic.'

'There's only one thing for it,' my husband Jim had said, his green eyes surveying the bulky extrusion in my otherwise slight figure, 'you'll have to ask your sister if she can come up to take care of Sarah. I certainly can't take any time off.'

His mind obviously otherwise occupied, he'd pushed his fingers through his fair hair, and turned back to the newspaper while I arranged for my sister, Pat, to come.

When Sarah had been born, only thirteen months previously, I'd been taken into the nursing home as soon as the waters had broken and was made to stay in bed for the next two days until the contractions started. Determined not to repeat the experience, I now procrastinated as much as possible, asking the nursing home staff if I might have a bath before coming in.

'Most definitely not!' matron's voice boomed down the phone, at which point I went suddenly and violently into labour. This baby was, evidently, in more of a rush to make her presence known.

Gathering up my suitcase, I took a last look at Sarah's sleeping face. Then it was out to the car, the warm summer evening slipping into the darkness of night as we made our way to the nursing home.

Jim took me in, making teasing protestations about the inconvenience of my timing. 'You do realize I'm missing prime drinking time, don't you?' he joked. 'You'd better get a move on, or I shan't be able to wet the baby's head tonight.'

Preoccupied with the events of the next few hours, I took it all in good part, though there had been underlying conflict regarding this pregnancy. Jim and I had been so young when we'd married, and had had little time together before Sarah's birth. She'd been only four months old when I'd conceived again, and Jim had accused me of manipulation.

He made constant reference to feeling trapped, but far from having engineered things, I'd had no desire myself to be in this state again so soon. It was true, I'd always said I wanted babies, and lots of them, but there had barely been time to enjoy the first before being launched back into early morning sickness and backache once more.

My health had deteriorated along with our relationship, so it was not in a happy frame of mind that I was driven through the city streets and checked into my room. Though I'd spoken to the staff myself to warn them of the imminence of my arrival, the nurses could hardly believe the advanced state of labour which had so quickly followed. There was no time for the normal premed. Within the hour Vicky was born.

If there had been any reluctance on our part as parents to bring this child into the world, for me, at any rate, it completely evaporated with her arrival. Vicky was the image of her father. To look at her was to see him in miniature. The same bone structure was evident, the same features and expression.

'She's gorgeous,' I told my mother on the phone. All thoughts of how unwanted this pregnancy had been were banished in fond maternal pride.

'Don't forget you've got another one at home,' she reminded me gently, 'And she's gorgeous too!'

There was no need, in fact, to chide me. Though I loved both babies equally, it was immediately evident on my return home that I was dealing with a very different personality in Vicky. And it wasn't always a very comfortable experience.

My mother-in-law took up residence with us for a short time, since she had recently been widowed. Young and naïve as I was, having only just come of age, I found myself easily influenced by her strong personality. Where an easy-going affection and informality existed in my close-knit family, Jim's was steeped in a public-school tradition. Though the niceties of life were observed when necessary in my home, they were never allowed to intrude. The sort of protocol advised by my mother-in-law was thus complete anathema to me.

'You can't feed the baby in front of Debbie,' she chided when our mother's help returned. 'It just isn't the done thing.'

What she meant was that I was not to feed the baby in front of herself and Jim. We had only the one sitting-room, the greater part of our large old house having been divided off into flats, which we let. Instead of Debbie being asked to leave the room, I found myself banished to a cold, comfortless bedroom, without the companionship of my family around me.

Fearful of incurring her displeasure, I could hardly argue—especially since mother-in-law paid Debbie's

wages. Whether it was the tension produced within me
by this action, the cold, the feeling of being left out when
the family were all together, or the antagonism which
inevitably arose in me, is not clear, but it was certainly
not conducive to a relaxed relationship with my new
baby.

Despite her haste in making her entry into the world,
Vicky now made her presence felt in a very real way by
constantly falling asleep at the breast. Tickling her feet,
prodding her cheek—all attempts were quite unsuccess-
ful in awakening her to the need of taking nourishment,
but try to remove her from her comfortable position
and she would howl the place down.

Hours of my life were spent in that cheerless bedroom
trying to feed an infant who preferred to sleep. Each
feed-time ran in to the next, and since the two children
shared a room and Vicky cried all night, there was little
peace. Within a few months, the constant friction had
caused an abscess, and I was convinced, wrongly as it
turned out, that I had breast cancer.

Throughout her childhood, the problem remained,
and though the doctors and nurses at the baby clinics
told me to have a more relaxed attitude to Vicky's eating
pattern, it was hard to put into practice.

Sometimes she would eat nothing, unless I sat and
made games with her food. Every mouthful had to be
talked through, every teaspoonful had to become an
aeroplane looking for a tongue to land on, or a bear
needing a cave to hide in. It was exhausting and very
time consuming. And there was no guarantee that the
'airport' or 'cave' might not be closed down at the
moment of entry.

But to do nothing simply resulted in Vicky taking no
nourishment and throwing tantrums, unless it was food
of her choosing. In order to preserve my own sanity I
would sometimes leave her to get on with it, but the net
result was a well-fed dog since Vicky would empty the
contents of her bowl off the tray of her high chair to an
eagerly awaiting animal.

Nevertheless, Vicky was a tremendous source of maternal pride. She was the sort of baby that people crossed the road to croon over. Her father's extrovert personality was very evident in her little round face, and merriment sparkled in her eyes. Where Sarah was quiet and dreamy like me, Victoria had a mischievous quality which was apparent to all. But as she grew into the toddler stage, the feelings I had had from the time she was born became increasingly stronger. It was as if there were a power struggle between us. More often than not, I felt that it was heavily weighted in favour of my child, and that my attitudes, behaviour and way of life were dictated by her demands.

Jim had little time for family life. Engrossed in the intrigues of the business he was building up by day, he spent most of his evenings in the pub. This too was alien to my family's way of life, though in fairness to Jim he was not to know this at the outset. Our courtship had taken place largely within the context of a hard-drinking social life. This quickly palled for me, but with the advent of my babies it seemed that the only way to enjoy Jim's company was to join him whenever possible. That often proved difficult. Since we lived hundreds of miles from either his family or mine, baby-sitters were not always available. Increasingly my life became more lonely and more isolated.

Then catastrophe struck. It was one of those nights that are for ever remembered, if for no other reason than the state of the weather. We'd had near-blizzard conditions all day, and Jim had only been able to collect my sister, Pat, from the station in the Land Rover because of the chains on its tyres. Once more she had come in response to my need of help, since I was just getting over a really bad bout of flu and Sarah now appeared to have gone down with the same thing.

Pat took one look at the sleeping toddler, and immediately took stock of the situation, her grey eyes showing concern. 'That child has more than flu. Meggie, I think you really ought to send for the doctor.'

Reluctantly, in view of the inclement weather, I telephoned, running my fingers anxiously through my already tousled head of curls. 'She's unable to raise her head from the pillow,' I told the locum to whom I'd been connected.

'Do you realize what time it is?' he demanded. 'Can't it wait until tomorrow?'

I looked at my watch, embarrassed at having incurred his displeasure. It was eight-thirty. Outside, the snow drifted soft and white through the now still night air. Always a little fearful of authority, I was even more diffident as a result of my illness. How could I expect him to come in this?

'I can't possibly get up the hill in this weather,' he exclaimed irritably, as if reading my thoughts.

Beside me, Pat nodded her auburn head emphatically. Younger than me she might be, but on this occasion she'd assumed authority.

'My husband could come to collect you,' I replied weakly. Thank goodness he'd not gone out again after bringing Pat home.

The gritting lorries had done their work, all but clearing the main roads at least, but even so it was nearly ten o'clock by the time Jim arrived back. Anxiously, Pat opened the door to admit the two men amid a flurry of snow and stamping of feet.

'She's complaining of pains in her head,' she informed the doctor.

'Don't you know a simple case of headache?' he fumed when he at last completed his brief examination. Then turning to Jim, 'Your wife's just being rather neurotic, I'm afraid,' he said.

'She has been ill herself,' Jim demurred, following him out of the front door.

I'd barely got out of bed the following morning when my own doctor arrived. Gently he made his examination of Sarah, then raised his head gravely.

'I think she may have meningitis,' he said kindly, 'but I can't be sure, I'll need a second opinion, and we may

well have to take Sarah into hospital. Can you prepare a
suitcase in readiness?'

Within the hour he returned in the company of a
paediatrician, and shortly after that an ambulance was
sent for.

Jim was out of town on business. Dressing myself
warmly in a red woollen skirt, ribbed tights and boots, I
donned my sheepskin coat to accompany my little
daughter in the ambulance, leaving Victoria in Pat's care.

'Oh please, God, please, God,' I whispered incoher-
ently as I prepared to leave.

'P'ease, God, p'ease, God,' Victoria echoed behind me.

Like a nightmare, everything seemed to be slowed
down so that every detail was etched minutely in my
memory. Sarah, her blonde curls and ashen face con-
trasting vividly with the scarlet blanket in which she was
wrapped, was carried out carefully by a burly ambulance
man down the snow-covered drive to the waiting
vehicle.

'We think it may be meningitis,' the white-coated
medics echoed to me as they ushered me into a waiting-
room and wheeled my little daughter away. 'We'll have
to take lumber punctures to be sure.'

Fearfully I awaited the results, having no clear idea of
what to expect. Meningitis was a disease unknown to me.
After some hours I was joined by Jim, Pat having con-
tacted him, and together we were summoned into a tiny
office.

'Your daughter has encephalitis,' the house-doctor
said, stabbing his pen back and forth on the blotting pad
which covered his desk. 'That's inflammation of the
brain itself'—he must have seen the blank expression on
my face—'and it's caused by a virus rather than a bac-
terium.'

'Can you tell us what that means?' Jim asked, shrugging his shoulders.

'It means that by the time we culture it and identify it,
she'll either be dead or over it,' he told us as gently as
possible.

I felt numb. What had we done to deserve this? Sarah was a beautiful child—all peaches and cream. 'Please, God, please. . . .'

There was still Victoria to consider.

'You'll obviously have to spend most of your time here with Sarah,' Jim decided, a worried frown on his forehead as he took stock of the situation. 'Pat has to return to London within the next day or two. Would your parents have Vicky if I took her down?'

Without further delay, this was arranged. And so it was that at the tender and impressionable age of two, Vicky was unceremoniously dumped upon her grandparents, whom she had barely seen, several hundred miles from home. That they would love her and care for her I had no doubts. Sally, my youngest sister, was only eight years of age, so my mother was well used to the wiles and tantrums of a two-year-old; but without doubt, Vicky's personality was beyond the ken of anyone in my family.

Inevitably, with Sarah's life hanging in the balance, I was utterly preoccupied, and gave little thought to the effect that this sudden and lengthy estrangement might have on her sister. Had I but understood, or received counselling on the matter, I might have made her, too, the subject of my prayers.

These were the days when little was understood or acknowledged of a child's need of its mother at such critical times. Far from receiving any help or advice regarding other children in the family, mothers were not even permitted to spend the night in the hospital with the sick child. The staff who took care of Sarah were more enlightened than most, allowing me to spend the greater part of the day with her, so that she seemed to survive the trauma without undue emotional damage. But when, at last, the time arrived to take her home, it simply never occurred to me to consider our enforced separation as a possible factor in subsequent relationship problems with Vicky.

But God had been faithful regarding my eldest

daughter. Though not a committed Christian at the time, I'd begged him to give her back to me, and in my naïvity and arrogance, I struck a bargain with him. 'If you will heal her, Lord, I'll make sure she grows up knowing you,' I'd promised.

It wasn't entirely clear to me how this was to be carried out, but since Sunday school had figured in my own childhood, that seemed to be a good starting place. I'd 'asked Jesus into my life' when I'd been fourteen years old, as a result of reading a children's novel entitled *The Yellow Pup*. It had been awarded to my father as a Scripture prize in 1923, but there had been precious little understanding on my part since my family were only occasional church-goers. Nevertheless, God seemed to honour that commitment on my part, and though I'd gone right away from him during the ensuing years, he now used my children's attendance at Sunday school to bring me back. Though I had let go of him, he it seemed had never let go of me.

I'd passed the vicarage on numerous occasions, since it was only a few houses along the road from our own. Sunday school, for the under-threes, was held in its capacious dining-room, and was run largely by the Vicar's wife, Eileen, who herself had two children. As soon as Sarah was well enough, I took my two along to join the happy little throng who so enthusiastically clapped and sang choruses—they could almost be heard from our home.

That first Sunday, after I had scurried home, was spent in wall-papering—or ceiling-papering to be more precise. I had co-opted Jim to help, having done the rest of the flat myself alone, and I hoped, somewhat optimistically, that we might be finished before it was time to collect the girls.

As time went on, Eileen invited me for coffee on several occasions, and friendships grew up between the children and between ourselves. Gradually I began to discover an awakening interest in a God whom I had only vaguely known hitherto. The family services, to which I was invited, proved to be quite different from the formal, ritualistic experience of my childhood. Most of all was the growing realization that Eileen, with her quiet wisdom and strength, had something which was lacking in my own life.

When after some months she invited me to attend a Billy Graham rally, though it would be untrue to say that I jumped at the chance, I certainly had a desire to know more. The effect upon me of that great auditorium packed with people praising God is difficult to describe. I was only aware of a great urge within me to know God as they evidently did, and I had such a sense of unworthiness that when Billy Graham issued his invitation to come forward, I remained rooted to the spot. Undeterred, and unknown by me at the time, my faithful friend continued to pray, and ultimately at my request took me to a second meeting in another city. With her at my side, I made my commitment, once more asking Jesus into my life as my Saviour and Lord.

Already there was friction in my marriage, and my new-found faith seemed to exacerbate this. Jim's long hours at the office and pub-centred social life left little time for family recreation, and this was a constant source of conflict between us. Having come from such a close-knit family, I very much resented the years slipping by with no apparent prospect of a similar lifestyle for my children. I longed for them to know that same sense of security and acceptance as I had known.

Jim had seemed to adore Sarah when she'd been born, showing her off to all his friends as if she was a unique and unparalleled creation. And, or course, she was—though neither he nor I then knew the precious truth of Psalm 139, which speaks of God knitting us together in our mother's womb and knowing our unformed body before the beginning of time.

As a toddler Sarah had reflected the same intensity of feeling back to him, delighting in his company and creating endless games in which an imaginary 'Daddy' figured extensively. But from having been quite antagonistic about the prospect of a second child, Jim now suddenly switched his affections to Vicky. Little had been written about the psychology of parenting, and we were both young and naïve. It's doubtful that Jim realized the effect of his behaviour, but I can well remember remarking upon it one evening.

Sarah had been making a bed for her dolls, using the clean terry napkins as sheets and covers. The rare advent of Jim's arrival home before the children had gone to bed was heralded by her shrieks of delight as she turned from her task and rushed towards the door, her blonde curls bouncing and her eyes alight with joy. Wrapping her chubby arms around his leg, she asked to be lifted up. But Jim, ignoring her pleas, advanced into the room where Vicky seemed to be awaiting her moment.

Suddenly, with the timing of a veteran actress, our youngest daughter whipped one of the nappies from the chair, ejecting the dolls from their 'bed', and using it as a toreador might when tackling a bull in the ring, she waved it aloft. The triumph of the success of her attention-seeking tactics was written all over her little face, and both Jim and I burst into peals of laughter. She looked so funny and was so obviously playing up to her dramatic finale that I almost failed to notice Sarah's reaction. Her face had crumpled, all the joy and radiance of seeing her father replaced by a bewildered expression of hurt. How could we, she seemed to be saying, laugh so uproariously at her sister's vandalization of her dolls' bed?

When I later drew Jim's attention to the effect of our actions, he dismissed it as of no moment. And for some years Vicky was quite obviously his firm favourite, needing little encouragement but receiving plenty to entertain and delight him in an increasingly precocious manner.

3

Mummy's Little Monster

Always the life and soul of the party, as indeed was her father, Vicky became more and more a source of guilt to me. I simply had no idea what made her tick, and felt I had to turn a blind eye to many of her misdemeanours in order not to be constantly picking on her. Where a simple instruction met with obedience from Sarah, to Vicky it constituted a challenge.

'Don't touch plugs,' I would say, only to be met with a demand to know why? 'Because you can be electrocuted and it would hurt,' I would remonstrate.

Half an hour or so later, back she would come. 'I jest put plug in, an' I not 'lectocuted.'

Her tone of voice seemed to challenge any shred of authority in my position, but I dared not smack her too often, finding the contrast in her behaviour and that of Sarah too disturbing. What was it, I questioned myself, that was lacking in me thus to negate my capabilities as a mother?

I was busily engaged in one of my least favourite jobs one morning, polishing the brass knobs and fingerplates which constituted the door-furniture throughout our flat. I had just completed the edge of the mat-well at the front door, when there was a shriek from Sarah.

'Mummy, Mummy!' Her little round face was flushed

with concern, her big eyes opened wide. 'Come quick,' she grabbed my arm. 'Vicky taken nasty sweeties.'

The theme music was playing at the end of *Playschool* on the television. Without conscious thought my mind registered the time: eleven o'clock. Rising quickly from my knees and dropping my cleaning cloths on the floor, I flew into the kitchen. Vicky whirled guiltily at my approach, hiding her hands behind her back. On the floor lay a nearly empty pill bottle.

Investigation with one finger revealed that Vicky had, indeed, taken something: her mouth was full of sediment. Holding her upside down over the sink, I pushed my finger down her throat in an effort to make her vomit. She bit me, and smiled angelically. Quickly I mixed a solution of salt water and poured it into her mouth. She constricted her throat and spat it down my dress. Her iron will clearly needed more than my ineffective remedies. With her little body, squirming in protestation, tucked under one arm, I rang my doctor who advised me to take her into Casualty immediately. Somehow—perhaps by divine inspiration—I had the presence of mind to put what remained of the offensive tablets in my handbag.

On arrival at the hospital, we were shown into—amazingly—an empty waiting-room. A white-coated doctor took the tablets for analysis. Meanwhile, Vicky polished the floor with her bottom and examined the radiators to see if they could be dismantled. Sarah sat quietly on a chair.

The tablets were returned. Vicky asked to go home. A second member of staff took the tablets for analysis, returning them later, and then a third.

'Shouldn't somebody examine my daughter?' I asked tentatively. Forty minutes had elapsed since the end of *Playschool*, and though death was obviously not imminent, judging by the increasing volume of protest from one small daughter, it seemed to me that events were taking place in reverse order.

Eventually a stomach-pump was applied to the

patient, and the calmness with which I had dealt with the situation so far evaporated as it was taken out of my hands. As with Sarah's illness, I had been praying from the word go, though in this situation with a far better understanding and a personal knowledge of the Lord to whom I prayed. Again, as on that earlier occasion, Jim was out of town on business. It seemed that my dependence was to be on God alone.

'There's nothing alien in Vicky's stomach,' the nurse informed me as she returned my now screaming, scarlet-faced child to me. 'Are you sure you couldn't have been mistaken?'

'I *know* there was sediment in her mouth,' I explained, embarrassed at having evidently been thought to have wasted their time.

'Well . . . if you're sure. Perhaps you'd better take her over to Pathology.' They handed me a form, and we set off in search of the laboratories for a thumb prick. The decibels of protest from my little 'monster' increased: they had chosen her sucking thumb.

'Did her sister take any?' enquired the technician as he examined the slide under a microscope, 'They usually work in pairs. Mine did.'

What an encouragement it was to know that I was not alone in my guilt, that others had fallen prey to not having eyes in the back of their heads. Until now I had roundly condemned the parents of children who suffered the consequences of their 'neglect'. Now I understood, to my cost, just how easily and quickly it could happen.

The results were almost immediate as the technician lifted his head from the microscope. Vicky had absorbed all the drug into her bloodstream, though fortunately it had been only a mild painkiller, and there must, evidently, have been too little left in the bottle to have had much effect. Mercifully, at least for those of us with tender eardrums, sleep eventually came to the thwarted thumb-sucker.

The winter season, with its heavy falls of snow, was

always a delight to both little girls. We lived in a quiet road on a gentle slope and had a fairly extensive frontage. A small flat-bottomed toboggan, kept within the confines of our own front garden, should therefore have presented little problem. Bundled up in anoraks, scarves, woolly mittens and bobble hats, and with strict instructions not to venture out onto the road, Sarah and Vicky were allowed out to play. From inside, I would keep an eye on them from the lounge window.

'Now, don't talk to anyone passing by,' I would adjure them as, faces alight with joy, they ventured forth. 'Because they might take you away to be their little girls.' I continued in response to the perrenial why? Smiling fondly I would return to my housework in the sure knowledge that Sarah, though only a year Vicky's senior, would automatically assume a parental role should the latter take it into her head to do anything silly. On one occasion, however, it was Vicky herself who, with great pride and as soon as an opportunity had presented itself, rushed back to inform me: 'I talked to a stranger, and he didn't take me away.'

The pressures grew. I loved my little daughter dearly, and felt a tremendous surge of pride in the very obvious pleasure others had in her company. But the fact that she exerted such a fascination, not only upon her nursery-school friends, but also their parents, only served to make me feel more and more inadequate.

Fathers especially, returning her from their child's birthday party, would make a point of telling me how much they had enjoyed her 'performance'. 'I haven't laughed so much in years,' said one. 'She should be on the stage,' said another.

Her nursery-school teachers soon learned how not to handle her. 'Now then, children, shall we sing the Jesus song?' one asked, during a nativity play to which the parents has been invited. Vicky, her angel's halo slipping over one eye, smiled sweetly and innocently. 'No thank you,' she said, walking off stage.

Her very first school report issued when she was only

three years old, read: 'A very intelligent little girl. . . . She is very popular with the other children.' And a year later: 'A very bright and intelligent child. . . . Vicky is always anxious to be "doing". She is most enthusiastic and interested . . . a joy to have in a class.'

As her school days progressed and she moved into primary school, Vicky became increasingly popular among her peers. Put her in an empty playground, or alone on the beach during the summer holidays, and within no time she would be surrounded by children. Without saying a word, her magnetism seemed to work on others.

A constant stream of 'boyfriends' beseiged her from an early age with gifts, telephone calls and protestations of undying love. A natural tomboy, she revelled in their company, accepting their gifts with enthusiasm but keeping them firmly in their place. She was, to her own mind, quite simply 'one of them'. Yet she was equally able to form close relationships with girls too.

Only at home did she resort to the cat as her comforter and friend, confidante and companion. Usually a bustling and active little girl, she had her father's capacity to 'switch off' instantly, often falling asleep wherever she happened to be. One moment she would be noisily engaged in playing some game or other with great gusto, in the next she was to be found curled up on the floor, thumb in mouth, dead to the world. Frequently she would have one arm draped around the cat, and I would sometimes come across her whispering secrets to this best-loved of our animals.

And there was a real need in her life for comfort and support. Constantly 'in the wars', we eventually discovered that Vicky had an eye condition such that she could only see through one eye at a time. Her perception of distance and depth was thus deficient, causing her to make frequent misjudgements when it came to jumping from a height or avoiding objects in her path.

For several years we frequented the hospitals, spending the greater part of the day awaiting a ten-minute consultation with the specialist's assistant's underling. Throughout her primary-school years, Vicky had to wear a patch, first on one eye, then on the other, in order to counteract the dominance of either. She hated it. Especially when, with the cruelty seemingly inherent in all children, she became known by various unflattering nicknames. Yet always there seemed to be this natural capacity for making others laugh, and her quick wit could size up a situation with a succinctness beyond her years. She was quick, also, to take advantage of others' gullibility, and her dry manner of presentation left you wondering just who had been taken in by whom.

'These sheep are dirty, aren't they, Mummy?' Sarah once remarked as we made our way across the moors en route to the dog kennels. 'They're not nice and white like Gran and Gramps' sheep.'

'Silly,' Vicky retorted, quick as a flash, tongue in cheek. 'You don't expect Mr Taylor to have time to look after all the dogs *and* bath the sheep every night, do you?'

But what had been cuteness in a small child ceased to be attractive as she grew older, and a wit which was often at the expense of others' feelings began to be seen as an undesirable and embarrassing trait. We had done Vicky no service in our attitudes towards her: her father in actively encouraging her, and me with my guilt-ridden lack of discipline.

Kate, a close friend as well as being Vicky's godmother, though she was not a Christian, had chosen both children to be her bridesmaids. Her well-to-do parents had erected a huge marquee on the lawns between the rose beds, not far from the swimming pool in front of their large country house. The official photographer was obviously in his element in having so attractive a choice of backdrops against which to arrange his subjects. He had not bargained, however, for the likes of Vicky.

She was hungry. Photographs could wait; food could not. The photographer patiently and politely cajoled and amused her—all to no avail. He would obviously cheerfully have omitted her from the group settings, but Kate was determined that her godchild should grace the pictures, come what may. Being a girl to whom protocol meant little in comparison to people, she provided Vicky with a large bread roll and insisted that the photographer proceed.

A bridesmaid whose chubby face, stuffed with bread and smeared with butter, is preserved for perpetuity on film, may make a good talking-point, but I found these demonstrations of Vicky's wilfulness excruciatingly embarrassing. However, to deal with it by smacking, or removing the child often increased the embarrassment. Add to this my constant feelings of picking on her, and guilt over the contrast in my dealings with Sarah, and I seemed not to be doing too well in my chosen career of motherhood.

In great concern, I spoke to our family doctor.

'I just don't seem to be able to handle her,' I told him, anxiously twisting a handkerchief in my lap. 'She seems to be getting more and more out of control, and Jim is so rarely at home, he does nothing to help.'

'She just needs more love, Mrs Scott,' he replied. 'There's obviously insecurity there, and the only way to deal with it is by making a real effort to let her know you love her.'

'But I do love her, Doctor. It's not an effort,' I looked up indignantly. 'She's never been an affectionate child,' I continued, casting my mind back. 'Even as a tiny baby, she hated being kissed and cuddled. But I feel as if she's testing me all the time to see how far she can go.'

'Well, I can only repeat—she needs more love.' He picked up his pen, indicating that the interview was at a close. 'Forget the discipline. She's just a spirited child, and you don't want to break that spirit.'

I wasn't so sure about that. The 'spirit' he spoke of was hardly conducive to harmonious relationships at home or abroad. To me, it seemed more like a spirit of disruption.

I shared with both Jim and Kate my fears and doubts.
Jim still very obviously applauded Vicky's vivacity, and
made odious comparison with Sarah whom he called a
'goody-goody'. To her face he gave her the nickname
'Creep', and this had the effect of polarizing us. The
more he turned against Sarah and encouraged Vicky,
the more I felt the need to take the part of our eldest
daughter.

It was an intolerable situation, and with a third baby,
Ruth, now added to our family, was beyond my en-
durance. Kate, who seemed to have a better understanding of Vicky than I, and who was not burdened
with feelings of guilt, could be more objective.

'I think she needs to be disciplined more consistently,
Meg,' she said, her hazel eyes screwing up in concentration. 'The thing is, you let her get away with murder
most of the time, then when it gets too much for you,
you come down on her like a ton of bricks. She just
doesn't know where she is with you.'

I thought long and hard about these recommendations. It was probably true. My parents had always been
strict disciplinarians with my sisters and me, yet we had
respected and loved them the more. We'd known the
boundaries—and the penalties if we crosssed them. It
seemed to me that this was rather like God's love for
us—firm and consistent, so that we know where we are.
Surely this is what gives us our sense of security? And
should we give any less to our children?

Certainly, I felt more inclined to go for this line of
reasoning than the doctor's. Vicky had to live within the
confines of society, and a certain measure of conformity
and consideration of others was necessary, not only for
my benefit, nor simply for convention's sake, but for
Vicky herself. It seemed to me that she was pursuing a
path of eventual self-destruction even then, in that her
popularity among her elders was very definitely in the
decline.

But the fact remained that there had been unity
between my parents not only in their discipline of my

sisters and me, but in every respect, and that was something which was sadly lacking betwen Jim and me.
Although during the months leading up to Ruth's birth,
and for a short time afterwards, we seemed to enjoy
probably the best part of our marriage, we were in reality poles apart in our outlook and expectations of life.

Jim's business had taken a new turn, expanding rapidly into new areas, so that he was frequently away for
days at a time. We'd moved house during my third
pregnancy, and passed through a sticky patch financially, having overstretched ourselves, all of which only
served to put an increasing strain on our relationship.

Then there was the question of my faith. Jim's initial
reaction to my commitment as a Christian had been mild
amusement. 'Oh, well, if you need something to lean on,
it might as well be that,' he'd smiled, pushing his fair
hair back from his forehead as I'd told him of my
experience.

As time progressed, he semed to view the children's
Sunday school attendance and my church-going with
the same rather condescending attitude, though from
time to time he would accompany us to family services.
But by and large his quest was for money, power and
pleasure, with family life taking a decreasingly smaller
proportion of his time and energies.

Together with my now closest friend, Eileen, our
vicar's wife, I prayed constantly that Jim would come to
know the Lord. My love for him was, if anything, more
intense than ever, and though our worldly way of life
caused me such internal conflict, I was careful to continue in order not to alienate him any further. But as the
girls progressed through primary school, the gulf between their father and me gradually widened. Jim
seemed to throw all consideration to the winds, often
not returning from the office, when he was not away,
until late at night after I had retired to bed.

On one such occasion when the rows had become so
frequent and so heated that it was obviously impossible
to go on any longer as we were, I found that I could

endure no more. The special meal I'd prepared was spoiled beyond redemption, and I'd had enough. Curiously, the heat and passion had gone from me, and it was in a calm and collected frame of mind that I packed my suitcase.

'I have to spend some time away from home to think things out,' I told Jim when he eventually arrived home, not unusually somewhat the worse for drink.

His face crumpled, his tall, lean frame seeming to shrink. 'I'm sorry, Meggie. I had to work late,' he excused himself.

'I've booked myself into a hotel overnight. We can't go on like this, and I've just got to get away to sort myself out.' I ran my fingers through my unruly curls.

'Then at least let me join you for a late supper,' he pleaded.

Reluctantly I agreed, and during the ensuing hours the reason for our strained relationship emerged.

'I've been having an affair,' Jim suddenly blurted out. 'Couldn't you guess?'

I felt as if the bottom had dropped out of my world. I adored Jim. How could this be happening to us? Feverishly, I begged the Lord to save my marriage.

For months the trauma dragged on. To begin with Jim begged me to return home, but having achieved this desire he then left the children and me to live with his girlfriend. The constant on-off situation took its toll, causing me so much stress that I came close to a breakdown and hospitalization. The children's welfare was beyond my capabilities as I wrestled with the implications of rejection, of being left alone for ever. Child of God or no, I did not handle it well. Eileen and Charles, my only close Christian friends, had moved away, and having been brought up in a family whose members, though very supportive, believed in keeping things of a private nature to themselves, I had no one else to turn to. Despite our closeness—or perhaps because of it—I could not share my predicament with my sisters and parents. I still loved Jim and hoped for reconciliation.

The fewer people who knew, I reasoned, the easier that reconciliation would be to achieve.

My inability to cope was reflected in the behaviour of both the older children. Sarah became more self-assuming than ever, adopting the 'little adult' syndrome which only served to alienate the sister she presumed to mother. Vicky's attitudes and school work deteriorated markedly. Within a year her test marks had dropped from around seventy-five per cent to less than half. The teachers' comments showed disappointment, not only in her lack of achievement but also in her increasing lack of interest and concentration. 'Poor mechanical result,' 'Seldom finishes a piece of work,' and 'Needs to make more effort' now replaced the previous expressions of pleasure and confidence on the part of her tutors.

When, after an unsettled eighteen months to two years, Jim suggested we move south to be nearer my parents, I felt I had little option but to agree. It would, he said, give us a better chance of making a new beginning. His affair, he assured me, was now over. And so it was that we made a fresh start. Vicky was just nine years of age, yet only five more years of innocence and childhood remained to her.

4

A Struggle for Supremacy

I sat in the car, feeling slightly stupefied by the heat of the sun which beat down on the roof turning the interior into a mini furnace. I didn't mind; the warmer the better as far as I was concerned. I'd always hated the cold, and for that reason, if no other, had been glad of our move from what my family termed 'the frozen north'.

Far below me, framed by conifers, the sea sparkled like gemstones. Closer at hand, nestling into the hillside, its red brick glowing in mellow harmony with the surrounding hollyhocks and rambling roses, was the convent.

We had chosen this place for Sarah's and Vicky's higher education for numerous reasons: the poor standards of the local comprehensive school; the good discipline offered by the nuns; the fact that other local children made the weekly pilgrimage, boarding Monday to Friday and then returning home for the weekend; and not least for its cosmopolitan flavour in an otherwise insular community.

Two years had elapsed since our move, when that choice had been made, and in the meantime the girls had attended the local primary school. Basking in the warm sunshine and drinking in the pine-scented air, I remembered how I had fought initially.

'I hate the idea of the girls going away to school,' I'd told Jim. 'I want them at home, here with me.'

'I know,' he'd nodded his head patiently. 'But we have to think of what's best for them.'

Somehow he made me feel as if I was being selfish. But it was all very well for him—he was away all week, commuting home at weekends only; I needed to feel of use to someone.

'Well, I feel a home life is best for them,' I'd said passionately. 'There's more to life than mere academic achievement.'

In the event, however, I'd had to accede. Drugs and promiscuity were rife at the local comprehensive according to Sally, my youngest sister, who, due to the closure of her own boarding school, had transferred to the sixth form. Only six years Sarah's elder, she was on the way out of secondary education as Sarah entered it.

The warm stillness was broken by the sound of a car engine starting up. All around, the lazy sounds of late summer changed to the low distant hum of children's voices. Roused from my reverie as the noise neared and increased in volume, I felt my body stiffen.

It was always the same. Inwardly I flinched, my muscles tightening up as if for fight—or flight? Mentally, I knew I was raising metaphoric arms to ward off the blows which would shortly be assailing me. More and more, I found myself dreading this time of the week, the pleasure of wanting to see and be with my children marred by the certainty of Vicky's verbal attacks.

'Mum!' Sure enough the strident tones of my middle daughter were launched through the air like a missile, long before she reached the sanctity of the car. 'Do you know what Sister Eloise has done now?' Throwing her suitcase into the back, she plonked herself down beside me. Absent-mindedly I winced. Now there would be a row. Sarah always complained of travel sickness in the back, asserting her right, as the eldest, to the front seat.

'No. What's happened now?' Soothingly, reining myself in, I made a great effort to smooth things down, past experience having taught me that this first hour could set the scene for the whole of the approaching weekend.

'She,' pointing an accusing finger in Sarah's direction as she trudged up the hill to the car, 'told her that they were her gloves when we had clothes inspection, so now I've got detention.'

Vicky always spoke very fast, as if afraid of losing the attention of her listener before she'd finished. As always, it took me some moments to sort out which 'she' constituted the subject of the sentence and which the object. Yet to delay too long before replying was to provoke further displays of temper. It was a *Catch 22* situation: you either risked an immediate, and possibly wrong response, or took your time over the interpretation.

'And were they Sarah's gloves?' I asked in trepidation, wondering if I'd successfully unravelled the mystery.

Vicky's round face broke into a sheepish grin. Struggling to maintain her air of hurt indignation, she shrugged one shoulder. 'That's not the point. I lent my gloves to Nina so she wouldn't get into trouble, but Fi chewed a hole in one, and then Nina said she couldn't find one, and anyway they weren't mine, they were Hazel's.'

Listening to the weekly tirade, one couldn't help but wonder what had gone wrong and how much was due to our home life. True, Jim had set up home with his girlfriend immediately we'd left the north, commuting between the two of us for six months or so until I'd found out. But I'd handled the discovery so much better on this occasion, finding a real trust and close walk with the Lord which had enabled me to cope so much more calmly. Apart from the fact of Jim's absence for a short while to consider my ultimatum that he choose between us, surely the girls could hardly have known what had happened? Yet there was no doubt, Vicky had an enormous chip on her shoulder. 'Everyone picks on me,' she would accuse. 'Why is it always me?'

'Do you realize, darling,' I ventured on one occasion,

'that you're the common denominator? Wouldn't it be a good idea to ask yourself if all those people 'picking' on you might not have good cause? Why don't you try to stop, take a deep breath, and just think what it is they're actually saying and whether there might not be a shred of truth in it, before launching into an attack?'

'Oh, you just don't understand,' she shrieked, her face suffused with anger. 'Sarah's your favourite. She's such a goody-goody. You just hate me.'

Try as I might, inevitably my patience would snap, and though without fail I refuted the allegations of hating her, reaffirming my love, I would find my voice rising and temper flaring. 'Please, Lord, help me to stay calm and show Vicky your love through me,' I would pray, aware of the fact that my own inner tensions were exacerbating the situation, inviting the expected response. Like Job I found that the thing I feared came upon me (Job 3: 25), so that the more I dreaded Vicky's attacks, the worse they seemed to get. It was almost as if, to coin the modern idiom, she 'picked up my vibes'.

Much of her behaviour, I was sure, dated back to the early days when precociousness had been fostered in her. But more than that, I was convinced, was the abrupt switching of attention on Jim's part once more—this time from Vicky back again to Sarah.

Throughout her childhood Vicky's cheeky and cheerful ways had dominated the scene, so that for ten years or so she had reigned supreme as her father's firm favourite. With the advent of our move south, however, Sarah had come back into her own. From infancy she'd been a veritable water baby, and in this one respect she was quite unlike me. Even into adulthood, my father teased me about my 'giraffe neck' when swimming. I couldn't bear water on my face, in my eyes or ears. Sarah, however, much to my horror and fascination, would lie in the bath fully submerged but for her nose, her eyes wide open beneath the water. A strong and fearless swimmer throughout her childhood, she would dive to the bottom of the baths for coins, and venture way out of her depth in the sea when visiting her grand-parents. Vicky, in this instance, shared my fear of water, and since during his bachelor days Jim had revelled in boating, it soon became apparent that this was to be the bone of contention.

One of the first things Jim accomplished once he'd made his choice between his mistress and myself—indeed, it may well have been the deciding factor—was to buy a largish boat with outboard motor. It didn't take long for Sarah's navigational skills to emerge, and it was almost a foregone conclusion that before the first summer was out a whole new relationship was forged between herself and her father.

Vicky was out in the cold. 'Throw that anchor out,' Jim would bellow as we approached one of the many beautiful beaches afforded us in this part of the country. 'No, you fool! You're supposed to hang on to the other end of the rope.'

With fear and misery written all over her face, Vicky would survey the anchor glistening alluringly beneath the waves, tantalizingly out of reach of the boat hook.

'Right. When I say "jump", jump,' Jim would instruct in an attempt to beach the boat on another occasion.

'No, you fool! You're supposed to take the painter and pull us in.'

'You fool' became Vicky's nickname, as 'Creep' had been Sarah's. No matter how I remonstrated, it was to no effect. Father and eldest daughter became insepar-able—often to the detriment of the rest of the family.

'Look at Ruth's face, Jim. She'd love to go with you.' I'd point out after a long day on the beach.

'Sarah's coming with me to put the boat away,' was his rejoinder as he dropped us off on the quay. 'Ruth's too young. Besides, we may call in at The Old Boar for a drink afterwards. I can't take Ruth.'

It seemed all wrong to me, as I trudged back to the car with the other two. Jim and Sarah would return an hour or so later to eat the meal I would have prepared. I hated Sarah being encouraged into this wordly way of life, but I knew I was on thin ice. Most of the pubs in our holiday-resort town had tables in the open air, and providing the older children only drank Shandy, the publicans turned a blind eye. Many of the local families seemed to spend a good deal of time in this way.

Jim blamed my reluctance, in this respect, on my 'religious fervour', and complained of my being 'boring'. Most of the spiritual content of my life had to be followed during the week when Jim was away. Not that there was much available in this respect—evangelical believers were thin on the ground, most of the churches following a dry ritualistic form of religion which was anathema to me.

Sarah had joined the parish church choir, closely followed by Vicky when she discovered that this meant being able to sit with the boys rather than next to me. I rather doubt that much in the way of worship or learning took place, judging by the notes and doodles which fell out of the pockets of her clothes on wash-day.

Those Christian women whom I did know, mostly living some distance from our hedonistic little town, arranged youth squashes in an attempt to show their offspring that they were not totally alone in Christendom. During the summer months these took the form of barbecues outdoors or in a barn, depending on the clemency of the British weather. In winter we met in one another's homes, each mother providing quiches, trifles or some other delicacy.

On one such occasion, the missionary cousin of our hostess, previously unknown to me or the girls, said that Vicky had a 'mouthful of threepenny bits which spewed out of her whenever she opened her mouth to speak'. This was not in any way intended as a hurtful remark made off the cuff, but seemed to come to him as if a word of knowledge or perhaps a discernment of something more sinister. Whatever it was, it remained with me constantly as something to be pondered.

As she entered her teens I became increasingly concerned about Vicky, and made numerous efforts to converse with Jim on the subject. To be fair, I think he realized himself that all was not right, but his solution to the problem was perhaps, in retrospect, not always advisable.

'I don't always feel comfortable with Vicky,' he confessed in a rare moment of insight.

'Oh? Why's that?' My voice registered surprise, 'I thought you two were so alike.'

'That's just it,' Jim pursed his lips, shrugging his shoulders in perplexity. 'She's too like me. I don't like seeing all my own faults mirrored so accurately.'

Poor Vicky. My heart went out to her. Sarah was just like me, but far from causing problems, this only served to bring us closer. I had always known what made her tick. But Vicky? She was a complete enigma. Somehow I rather doubted that having failed miserably during thirteen years or so of attempting to comprehend her, success would now suddenly be within my grasp simply because she had need.

Jim's answer was to spend money. This had always seemed to be his 'religion'—the thing in which he had most faith. A *Mirror* dinghy and membership of the yacht club were both denied to Sarah, for a time, in order that Vicky might feel 'special'. Until, that was, her fear of water became apparent.

Already the owners of a pony, we acquired a second— for Vicky's use. She never shared Sarah's passion for riding, and though she'd always had lessons, was always having to be nagged to exercise and groom the animal. Throughout her childhood Vicky had begged to be allowed to do and to have whatever Sarah did and had. But usually the acquisition of the actual privilege or gift did little or nothing to appease her.

'What would you like for your birthday, Vicky?' would usually be met with: 'What are you getting Sarah?' It was as if Vicky saw herself as inferior, and felt that in some magical way her sense of inadequacy could be compensated for in this way. The truth was that she was every bit as capable as Sarah, but taking life to be a joke, she buffooned her way through classes—whether academic or otherwise—and made no effort to succeed. Her school reports gave repeated evidence of this, and from all that Sarah later told us, comparisons were often made between the two. 'Why can't you be more like your sister?' Vicky would be asked by her teachers, within the hearing of others. Music lessons, however, proved an exception. Sarah had always played for pleasure, no duress having to be applied, and had sailed through her exams. Vicky, on the other hand, seemed thoroughly inept, despite an apparent desire to succeed. I happened to mention to her teacher one day, something to the effect that Vicky had had eye problems. 'It can't actually be cured,' I explained, 'but we did have a cosmetic operation carried out before moving south, so that the squint was corrected before she started her new school.'

'So in fact she still only sees with one eye at a time?' Miss Maple asked.

'That's right, though of course experience has taught her to judge distance and depth.'

'It would explain, though, why she can't see two lines of music,' Miss Maple said knowledgeably. 'Would you consider switching her to the flute so she only has one line to read?'

A flute was bought immediately, much to Vicky's delight. Not only did this constitute one-upmanship on Sarah, but it had cost a considerable amount and was hers exclusively. But our delight was short lived. Within a year or so Vicky's mouth was covered with herpes—cold sores as they are commonly known.

'They're caused by stress,' our doctor told me. 'Emotional upsets, wind, sun, a cold, any number of things can be the culprit.'

'Stretching your lips over your teeth to play a flute?' I asked, screwing up my face in consternation and disappointment.

'Yes, that could cause it,' the doctor affirmed. 'Once you have the virus it remains in the skin for the rest of your life, flaring up whenever there's stress.'

The flute lessons limped painfully onwards for a spell, gradually petering out.

In January of the following year—Vicky's thirteenth —we received a letter from one of her teachers, asking that we allow Vicky to accompany her and her daughter to Nigeria where her husband was employed in a teachers' college. It seemed the chance of a lifetime, and Jim readily agreed as Vicky begged and cajoled. Arrangements were made for Vicky to spend the Easter holidays with the family, and it proved to be a huge success. Her school-friend was also the middle one of three girls, so as well as being a most instructive trip in terms of 'seeing how the other half lives' in a Third World country where extremes of poverty and affluence exist side by side, Vicky was able to experience, first hand, the tensions and strains which exist in all families.

She arrived home, a little brown berry of a girl, laden with Nigerian 'goodies', among them several fertility masks and other trappings of witchcraft and black magic. I thought nothing of it at the time, and only years later had any misgivings.

In the meantime, severe and prolonged back trouble had put me in and out of hospital and caused further strain in my relationship with Jim. Like many men he had never been able to tolerate sickness, seeing it as a weakness, and since mine had necessitated nearly eight months' bed-rest on this sixth occasion in twelve years, life had not been easy.

The enforced bedrest had the effect, however, of drawing me closer to the Lord, deepening, though I was scarcely aware of it at the time, my spiritual perception. In the state of despair and utter helplessness into which I had fallen, he was my only hope. Only in hindsight did I recognize the perfection of the Lord's timing, the way in which he was to prepare me for future events. Cocooned in my bed, away from the pressures of life in general and domesticity in particular, it was as if I was being incubated, warmed and nourished by my absolute dependency on his provision, so that at the right moment the 'hatching' might take place.

The 'right moment' proved to be a visit made to Eileen as soon as my back would allow. Learning from her of the power available to Christians through the filling of the Holy Spirit, I lost no time in seeking the victorious life for myself. During the three days and nights of prayer which followed, I was to learn of the need to hand over to God all that I held most dear—my home, my children, my marriage. Then—and only then—did I receive blessing and infilling of a magnitude never before experienced, and a new strength to cope with all that was to come. My love for the Lord knew no bounds.

During the autumn Jim seemed to be abroad more and more on business, and began arriving home late even when he was in the country. Perhaps I should have recognized the symptoms having been through it twice before. Certainly there was little satisfaction in our relationship, but it simply did not occur to me to suspect that once again another woman might be the problem. By Christmas of the same year, our marriage had come to an end.

'I'll tell the girls,' Jim said emotionally on the fateful Christmas morning. As it happened, I chanced to walk in on him as he concluded his confession, and I was just in time to overhear Vicky's reaction to the news that her father had been having an affair with the wife of his best friend.

'Poor Tony,' Vicky said, turning away to stare blindly out of the window. For a moment both Jim and I stood, open-mouthed at her perspicacity. Of all who were involved in the drama, Vicky alone had homed in on the one person who was least equipped to cope with the situation. Within a year, Tony was to meet with a fatal accident.

The reaction of all three girls during the eighteen-month long litigation leading ultimately to the divorce of their father and me, was fairly typical. Most children

are concerned, naturally enough, with their own security. Ours were no exception. Each suffered and behaved
in her own individual way: Sarah, at fifteen, by her self-
imposed adult stance; Ruth, at only nine, by with-
drawing into a nervous state of emotional tension which
shut out all other relationships bar her obsessive love for
me. Vicky was Vicky, regressing further and deeper into
an aggressive attitude of antipathy which seemed, at
times, to encompass most of mankind. Her relationship
with me, never good at the best of times, deteriorated
markedly, and though she could be kind and loving,
showing tremendous insight and compassion on occasions, for the most part it seemed that she blamed me
for any and every misfortune which befell her.

That strength of character, that power struggle which
I'd sensed in her from infancy, now came to the fore
with renewed vigour. The eyes, whose malicious sense
of triumph so scornfully glinted back at mine whenever
I lost my cool, seemed not to be those of the little girl I'd
held in my arms fourteen summers ago. Increasingly I
became aware of a sense of Vicky being outside of my
control, and, what was more, an insidious perception of
being manipulated myself lurked just beneath the
surface.

The indwelling power of the Holy Spirit and the new
strength and power in my Christian life seemed to have
met a force if not equal to its own then at least of a
sufficiency to inflame an already difficult situation. Impotence, rage and frustration built up within me like a
pressure cooker builds up a head of steam. There were
times, in dealing with my daughter, that I felt I must
surely burst a blood vessel. Egged on by her goading, yet
for ever struggling as a Christian to rein in on my anger,
it seemed prudent on occasions to give in to her
demands.

'I knew I'd win,' she would shrug her shoulders non-
chalantly, evidently bored with the conquest when once
she'd achieved her purpose. 'I knew I could get you to
do what *I* wanted,' she would taunt, leaving me feeling

sickeningly used by the Enemy in a situation which was far from glorifying to God.

Inevitably, my nervous tension communicated itself to others. Certainly, it was apparent to my doctor when he called one day to see Ruth who was suffering some minor childish ailment.

'What's the problem, Meg?' he asked kindly, unleashing a torrent of pent-up emotion from me. 'I really think you should take Vicky to see a child psychiatrist,' he advised when I'd finished. 'She's obviously been badly damaged by the break-up of your marriage, and I think that harm will be irreparable if you don't do something about it soon.'

'A child psychiatrist?' I echoed in some alarm.

'There's nothing to worry about,' he smiled, taking my acquiesence as read as he scribbled a memo for himself. 'I'll write off straight away. All that they'll do is get Vicky to talk about her feelings and air her grievances. You've said yourself that you can't get her to do so.'

It all sounded so harmless. Certainly, it was true that Vicky seemed unable to talk things out with me. Whenever I'd tried to get her to open up, it had ended in a shouting match, serving no useful purpose. Could this be the answer? Would a psychiatrist be able to unravel the tangled confusion of my daughter's heart and mind? Dr Duffy made the alternatives sound pretty awful, 'irreparable damage' had been his words—it was quite the reverse that I wanted for Vicky.

Still, I wasn't so sure I liked the idea of a psychiatrist. Would he put weird ideas into her head? If only there was someone within the church to whom I could turn for advice.

5

On the Brink

Hunched over the steering-wheel, I screwed up my eyes in concentration. It was almost impossible to discern the road ahead as I peered through the darkness and the rain. The windscreen wipers flipped back and forth at double speed, but despite their effort and the fact that I had slowed right down, visibility was virtually nil.

Sweat broke out on the palms of my hands as I gripped the wheel, and the car felt suddenly airless. Unable to stand the noise and heat a moment longer, I reached forwards and switched off the fan. In minutes the screen had misted over. Sighing fractiously, I switched it back on.

'Well,' I said peevishly, 'I haven't the remotest idea where we are.'

'I shouldn't think it makes much difference now, anyway,' Vicky replied, her head turned away from me as she gazed unseeingly out of the passenger-door window.

'What do you mean by that?' I asked crossly.

Momentarily she turned back towards me. 'We're so late now for the appointment, I shouldn't think they'd see us anyway.' She paused, then burst out accusingly, 'I don't know why you think I need to see a shrink anyway. I'm not a head-case, you know!'

My irritability melted away. Reaching out a hand, I put it on Vicky's knee, squeezing gently. 'I know, love. I don't think you're a head-case. Dr Duffy just thought it would help if you could talk to someone outside the family.'

Vicky pulled away, dislodging my hand. 'There's nothing to talk about.' Shrugging her shoulders, she turned back to the side window. Even from that angle I could see that her face was set in a hard scowl.

It was my fault that we were lost. Dr Duffy had made this appointment some months ago, back in the autumn, but I had only half registered the address on the top of the letter. I'd collected Vicky from boarding school, travelled the twenty miles or so to the town, and then headed straight for the hospital, assuming that the clinic, which went under the same name, would be under the same roof. By the time we'd traversed the town in an effort to correct the error, we were nearly an hour late.

Our late arrival didn't put me in a good light with the psychiatrist, Dr Sellick, nor with his receptionist. He had left for home some time earlier, she explained in haughty tones, while she had had to await our arrival, the hospital having telephoned ahead. It was, therefore, with a double dose of anxiety that I contemplated this interview, once a second appointment had been made for the following day.

It seemed to me that my fears were well founded as I surveyed Dr Sellick next day. His face was small and pinched, his pointed and upturned eyebrows, his eyes and the wings of hair at his temples giving him the appearance of a pantomime Diabolus.

Vicky had once again made her feelings known to me in no uncertain terms. Confronted by the doctor, she now simply clammed up, refusing to answer him in anything more than a monosyllabic fashion. It was left to me to fill the silence. It was hardly the sort of interview I had envisaged, and hesitantly I pointed out that Vicky might find it easier to open up in my absence.

'Perhaps on another occasion,' the doctor drawled, leaning back in his chair and bobbing gently back and forth on its pedestal rocker. 'I particularly want to see you both together to begin with.'

Vicky skulked low in her chair, her scowling face practically hidden in the upturned collar of her blazer.

'Can you tell me, Victoria, in what areas you feel your mother most restricts you?' Dr Sellick tipped his pointed little head on one side, his elbows on the arms of the chair, a pencil suspended between the fingers of each hand.

Lit by the arc of a single desk lamp, Vicky shrugged her shoulders, staring insolently back at him for a moment before averting her gaze. 'Ask her,' she replied at last, nodding in my direction. 'She's the one who wanted to see you.'

Dr Sellick nodded his head slowly, his neck and shoulders following suit, his eyes still on Vicky. Tipping his head suddenly to the other side, he switched his attention to me. 'Perhaps you can tell me, Mrs Scott?'

'I've forgotten what the question was,' I replied, feeling rather foolish.

'What do you see as the major areas of disagreement between yourself and Victoria?' His voice was smooth and honeyed.

'Well . . . .' Defensively I fidgeted in my chair, uncrossing my legs and sitting more upright. 'It's difficult to say really.' When you boiled it all down, it sounded so petty. What on earth were we really doing here, I wondered. Was it really going to serve any useful purpose?

Dr Sellick reached out and opened a file on his desk, extracting the single letter, and reading from it briefly before turning his attention back to me. 'Do you approve of Vicky's friends?' he asked. His smooth tones and langorous movements were beginning to get on my nerves.

'Not all of them,' I admitted. One up-pointed eyebrow lifted slightly. 'Well,' I rushed on defensively, 'it's not that I disapprove, it's just that . . . Vicky does seem to choose friends whose parents have . . . loose morals.'

'Can you explain that?' The doctor balanced the pencil between the forefinger of each hand.

'I just don't like her staying overnight with one girl whose mother has a live-in-boyfriend in the house.' I looked him straight in the eye, then dropped my gaze.

'I see. And how do you feel about that, Vicky?' The chair swivelled slightly in her direction.

'I can't see any harm in it,' Vicky replied harshly. 'Nessie's mum's been living with Vince for ages. They've probably got a better relationship than lots of married people.' She glanced accusingly at me, and I flushed as the psychiatrist also looked my way.

'I don't want my children growing up thinking that living together is the norm,' I said hotly.

'Are you saying that men and women shouldn't live together?' Dr Sellick asked.

'Not if they're not married.' I explained. 'As a Christian, I believe God intended sex to be kept within marriage. I know people do go off the straight and narrow . . . but to flaunt it openly . . . .'

'Ah! so if it's kept hidden it's all right?' The doctor rose from his semi-reclining pose to lean forwards in his chair.

'No,' I frowned, fidgeting in consternation. 'That's not what I meant . . . .'

'But your religious beliefs are such that you view sex as something sinful?'

'Only if you're not married. . . .'

'What about love?' Vicky stirred in her chair as the doctor regarded me intently. 'Vicky is obviously crying out for love. Supposing she had a boyfriend who genuinely loved her. Would you deny her the expression of that love?'

'As a Christian . . . .'

'Yes, Mrs Scott? As a Christian. . . ?' He straightened in his chair, leaning back once more. 'I would suggest to you, Mrs Scott, that perhaps you are, shall we say, a little . . . . fanatical? Most people these days have more relaxed attitudes towards sex. It is, after all, a healthy and wholesome outlet, and its repression can do untold damage. Perhaps you have some hang-up?' The corners of his mouth lifted in a smile. 'I don't mean to open old wounds, but didn't your husband, er, leave you for another woman?'

'I don't have any hang-ups,' I protested, scarcely able to believe my ears.

'Let's leave that for now,' the doctor said smoothly changing the subject. 'What about school? You mentioned earlier about Vicky wanting to leave school?'

Taking a deep breath to steady my nerves, I nodded agreement.

'What to you feel about that Mrs Scott?'

'I'd like her to stay on and get some qualifications,' I said, feeling on safer ground. Surely he couldn't fault me here.

'Have you given any consideration to her request to leave as soon as possible?'

'She's only fourteen and a half,' I gasped. 'She can't leave until she's sixteen anyway.'

'Fifteen,' Vicky interrupted coldly. 'You can leave as soon as the exams are over if your sixteenth birthday comes in the holidays.'

'And what then?' I whirled on her. Vicky always seemed to have an answer for everything.

She shrugged a shoulder, 'I can leave home then.'

'What about a job?' I asked, wondering how I'd ever got into this situation.

'There's always the dole,' her chin came up defiantly. 'Or I could get a job with Nessie. We're going to have a flat together anyway.'

'You won't earn enough in a shop to afford a flat,' I retorted.

'But you'd be agreeable to Vicky leaving school if she could get a job?' Dr Sellick enquired.

'I don't want her working in a shop,' I said, aghast at the way things seemed to be going.

'Why not?' the doctor regarded me from beneath the

eyebrows.

'Vicky's a clever girl. All her school reports say so.' Patiently I tried to explain. 'What a waste to end up in a shop when she could get some decent qualifications.'

'So basically you feel that shop work is not . . . shall we say . . . quite what you would expect a member of your family to be doing?'

'That's not what I said.' I felt sick inside. Every reply I made seemed, somehow, to be twisted. Was I on trial? Dr Sellick had glanced at that letter in the file on more than one occasion. What was it that Dr Duffy had written?

'There's nothing wrong with shop work,' I continued, silently sending up a little prayer. 'But I think Vicky would be bored to tears in no time. She could never sit still for two minutes from the time she was little, and I can't see her lasting long cooped up in a shop.'

'But you have to let your children choose for themselves, wouldn't you agree, Mrs Scott?' The doctor's honeyed tones, seemingly implying that non-agreement would constitute bigotry on my part, then continued in such a way as to bear out my theory. 'We can't tie our children to our apron-strings, can we? And surely we've all grown out of those Victorian attitudes of repressing our children's development, whether it be through sexual freedom of expression or any other way?'

It was in a state of some considerable confusion that I eventually stumbled out of the clinic into the dark of the night to seek refuge in the privacy of my own car. My hands were shaking as I started up the engine, and for some time I drove in silence. Vicky matched my mood, still staring out of the side window.

'Well!' I ventured, at last. 'What did you make of that?'

'I told you I wasn't round the bend,' she said in a softer and more pleasant tone than before. 'But if you ask me, *he* was.' She laughed briefly and scornfully. 'The psychiatrist that needs psychoanalysing—he was weird!'

'I couldn't agree more,' I said in some relief, glad to have an ally at last.

'All that stuff about me wanting to have sex,' she snorted derisively. 'I never even mentioned sex. P'raps that's where he gets his kicks.'

'Well, I wonder where that leaves us now?' I said, thinking aloud.

'Oh, Mum, please don't send me back there again.' Vicky turned passionately towards me, her voice pleading and slightly tearful. 'You won't, will you? Please!'

'No,' I negotiated a bend in the road. 'I think you're right. When the next appointment comes through, I'll tell them it's not convenient.'

'What about Dr Duffy?' she asked plaintively.

'Oh, don't worry,' I replied with more of an air of bravado than I felt. 'I'll tell him that we're certainly not going back to see a man who puts such suggestions into the heads of his patients.'

Even so, as I drove home later, after dropping Vicky back at school, I wondered if I would have the nerve. It seemed to me that Dr Duffy may well have been in cahoots with Dr Sellick. Certainly the latter had referred often enough to the letter from my GP, and it had not gone unnoticed on my part that it was only after his initial scrutiny that he'd launched into an attack of my faith.

Could there be any element of truth in his accusations, I wondered? Had I been imposing my spiritual convictions on Vicky in such a way as to alienate her, not only from myself, but also every other member of the family? If I had 'thrust religion down her throat', as the psychiatrist had implied, that would also make sense of why she rebelled against the nuns at school. But it didn't explain her aversion to her grandparents and aunts, since none of them had a practising faith.

Still the question remained. Had I—did I—impose a religious, legalistic concept of Christianity on my children? It had to be admitted that for many years I'd imposed perfectionist standards on myself, and it was only in the last two years that I'd known the real freedom for which Christ had died. It was on that occasion,

shortly before my marriage had come to an end that I'd
received the infilling of the Holy Spirit and had a whole
new experience of the Lord. I'd underlined Galatians
5:1 in my Bible: 'It is for freedom that Christ has set us
free.'

But the legalism—if that's what it was—that I'd experienced prior to that second touch, had been more in
the form of a personal sense of condemnation. And that
had come about precisely because I wasn't living up to
biblical standards as I understood them. It had not been
a question of living in a legalistic manner when I was
married to Jim, but quite the reverse. The conflict—and
there had been plenty—had all been internalized.

It was a problem which still plagued me. I longed for
my children to know Jesus as I did; to love him so much
that to follow him was joy, to depart from him sheer
misery. But though *I* had been relieved of that conflict
of having a foot in either camp, the girls were still very
much involved with their father and his way of life. The
dilemma which had faced me regarding Vicky staying
overnight with her friend Nessie, was still very much an
issue with Jim. Until such time as our divorce was final-
ized, he was living with Tony's wife, and I was loathe to
expose the girls to the reality of this.

'Be reasonable, Meg,' Jim said in exasperation during
one particularly heated telephone conversation prior to
the settlement of our divorce. 'It would make sense for
the girls to stay overnight when they come to see me. I
shall be marrying Sheila eventually.'

Rightly or wrongly, I'd stuck it out and insisted that
until such time as he and Sheila were married—if indeed ever—the girls should not stay with him. In every
other way I encouraged access, knowing it was for their
best to keep up a relationship with their father.

Jim, however, didn't see it this way. 'I hope you're
prepared for a fight,' he said cuttingly down the telephone. 'I shall be bringing in a London barrister to revoke the custody order.'

'I don't think you'll get far,' I replied, stung by his

attitude.

'You'd be surprised,' he retaliated. 'It seems that you're hardly considered a fit mother.' His voice took on a taunting, scornful quality. 'Did you know Dr Duffy's heard from the psychiatrist?'

My hands were shaking by the time I put the instrument down. Relationships had been particularly bad between Jim and me for some time, and I'd deliberately asked Dr Duffy to let *me* know the results of Dr Sellick's initial assessment, assuring him that I in turn would let Jim know. Surely he couldn't have gone behind my back in this way? Realizing that I should give the doctor the benefit of the doubt, I said nothing to anyone else but rang the surgery to make an appointment. In the small community in which we lived, one met up constantly with one's GP in social situations, and we'd all been on Christian name terms since we'd moved. It just didn't seem feasible that he would behave in this manner.

Just in case, however, I wrote a brief letter to the Medical Council, asking, for personal reasons, to be transferred to another doctor in the practice. If Dr Duffy had done as Jim implied, I would find it difficult to trust him again as my doctor and mentor.

'Jim tells me that you've heard from Dr Sellick,' I began, when I'd been ushered into his room.

'Yes,' he admitted somewhat guardedly.

For a moment I stared, in disbelief. 'And is it true that he feels I am an unfit mother?'

The doctor banged his pen down on his blotter. 'I told Jim not to tell you that,' he said in exasperation.

'So it's true?' My heart was hammering away somewhere in the pit of my stomach and I was finding breathing rather difficult. 'Did you know that Jim's intending to use that against me to take the children away from me?' My eyes filled with tears and my bottom lip trembled. I swallowed hard, feeling betrayed. 'You know I asked you to let me know the results first.'

'I have to do what I consider best for my patients,' he replied defensively.

'But Vicky and I are your patients, not Jim,' I said accusingly.

Thinking about it later, it still seemed unbelievable. I'd shown Dr Duffy the letter I had written to the Medical Council, and explained that since his loyalties seemed to be split, I felt it would be better to sign up with one of the other doctors.

In the event, when the decree eventually went through some eight or nine months later, no mention was ever made of Dr Sellick's letter, and neither did Vicky or I ever see him again, though numerous attempts were made to put pressure on me to do so.

I was concerned about the impression that Jim's way of life might have upon the children: moral attitudes, the use of alcohol, money and his priorities were not lost on them, and it seemed that they often found their visits with him vastly more enjoyable than time spent with me.

'Lord, I'm so concerned about his influence on their young lives,' I prayed one evening. And not without justification. Already there was evidence to show how their minds were being directed.

'Poor thing,' I'd overheard one of them remark one evening while watching television.

'Who's that?' I asked absent-mindedly from my ironing-board in the kitchen.

'This man,' came the reply. 'His wife is horrid—won't let him go to be with the lady he really loves . . . .'

I'd been horrified, and now, faced with the fact that even though I banned overnight stays, Jim still brought Sheila along at times, I had visions of the three girls growing up believing in the desirability of the so-called 'freedom of sexual expression' which Dr Sellick and his like promulgated so avidly. It was only wives like myself, and husbands like Tony, who knew the misery and pain meted out by these revolutionaries advocating 'open marriage'.

It was therefore with a heavy heart that I prayed, pondering as I lay in bed just what the future might hold for the three young girls whom I loved so dearly and whose lives had been so shattered. Into my mind came a clear picture of a seashore, the waves gently lapping the sands. On the water's edge Sarah, Victoria and Ruth were paddling. As I watched, the three were lifted in a net and hung suspended for a time while the salt water and weed fell away. Above them hovered a huge hand, and by and by, gently and in orderly fashion, they were lifted one by one and placed in its palm.

I knew that the Lord was showing me the past and the future. The paddling signified the fact that all three had experienced a walk in the Christian life through my faith and teaching. The net was to show that they would be caught up by the Fisher of men, and that by and by, when all the dross and impurity of their past life had fallen away, leaving them free and unfettered, their lives would be hidden in Christ himself, and their names written on the palm of his hand.

The significance of this vision—for that was what I understood it to be—was not lost on me. God had been gracious enough to give me a glimpse of the future. No matter what might befall them in the days, months and years to come, I knew that ultimately they would be safe with him. This was a vision to sustain me through whatever lay ahead.

6

Out of My Reach

Early the following year, Vicky's appearance and behaviour at school deteriorated considerably, and several
letters concerning her future passed between the nuns
and myself. It was with great consternation that I read
one from the Headmistress:

Dear Mrs Scott
  Your daughter, Victoria, has admitted to smoking on the
premises, which is strictly forbidden, as the girls all know. It
is strictly forbidden because of the danger to lives in these
buildings which have a lot of wood in their make-up, apart
from the fact that it is bad for their health.
  Instead of suspending girls for a week, in future they will
be fined £1 *out of their own pocket money* . . . . *She* must be
made to feel it, and not you. Previously, after the first
offence and a week's suspension, I have just expelled them
if it has occurred again.
  I hope you will make clear to Victoria the seriousness of
the matter. What I intend for the future is the next time
they are caught, it will be a fine of £5, and after that
expulsion.

A good deal of serious talking took place between us
all, with the result that by the end of the spring term a
further letter arrived indicating that Vicky had settled

down, with great improvement evident in both her appearance and her attitude towards work. The summer of that year saw the finalization of my divorce and Jim's immediate marriage to Sheila, now widowed since Tony's demise. Though they had been living together throughout the eighteen months or so of litigation, Jim now took on, in legal terms as least, the parenting of Sheila's three boys. Their claim on his time, money, discipline and affection did not pass unnoticed by the three girls, especially when the youngest boy, obviously suffering a sense of insecurity himself, seemed to delight in calling *their* father 'Dad'.

My relief regarding Vicky was short lived, and as the summer term progressed, it became obvious as her behaviour regressed once more that she was intent on doing all in her power to get herself expelled from school.

Her rudeness at home became unendurable, extending not for the first time to other members of the family. Driven to the end of his tether by her insolence towards both himself and me on one particular occasion, my father lashed out and spanked her. It was only a single smack, but the effect was instantaneous. Though pure hatred was evident in Vicky's eyes at this violation of her person, a hint of respect was also to be seen.

Once the tears and tirade had cooled, I was able to talk with Vicky, sitting on the edge of her bed as she lay sprawled across it.

'You seem to hate us all—me, your father, your sisters, and both sets of grandparents.' Sadly I surveyed her flushed face, its youthful fullness set firmly in lines of hate and aggression.

'What sort of a family life have I ever had?' she shouted angrily, her eyes flashing like emeralds. 'Every weekend when Sarah and I came home, you and Dad would be at one another—rowing. What d'you expect?'

'Well, darling . . . .' tears welled up in my eyes as I silently acknowledged the truth of her accusation, 'I'm sorry about that; but I can't change it. I wish I could.' Reaching out I put my hand on her shoulder, aware as I did so of the way she recoiled. 'Your father and I haven't lived together for the past eighteen months,' I continued. 'Isn't it time you tried to get over it? These rows between you and me are helping to create the same sort of atmosphere for Ruth to come home to.'

Though chastened, Vicky was far from contrite, clinging always to her past experience as the reason for all present behaviour.

'Don't you see, darling,' I ventured, 'you can choose how to behave. You don't have to let the past dictate to you. Look at Winston Churchill. He was an absolute dunce at school, but he put all that behind him and went on to become a great statesman.'

Vicky was unimpressed. 'What's that to do with me?' she demanded. 'You don't know how I feel. You don't even care.'

Unable to make any headway, and realizing that she was still in a highly volatile and belligerent mood, after much consideration I eventually told her that she was to stay at school the following weekend.

'We can't keep going on like this, Vicky,' I said, my hands still shaking with emotion. 'I think you'd better spend the next couple of weeks trying to sort out your feelings for your family and home. You seem to hate being here with us, so perhaps it would be better to stay away for a while.'

The next fortnight was a misery to me, the fourteen days seeming to stretch on interminably. Hating myself for putting Vicky through this period of discipline, I telephoned her several times. On the first Friday, when it was my turn on the rota to collect the other youngsters from school, I took up a supply of home-made strawberry mousse so that she would at least have some reminder of the love at home.

'Staying at school isn't meant to be a punishment,' I pointed out. 'I miss you dreadfully, and it hurts me to be firm with you, as much as it does for you on the receiving end.'

'I wish she had some trustworthy person to whom she

could talk,' I wrote once more to the Headmistress. 'She has put up so many barriers that it is quite impossible to show her any love, and she is utterly contemptuous when I tell her that I love her.'

Sister replied assuring me of her prayer support, but a letter received from Vicky during the same week intimated that the trauma had had little effect on her.

'I had a boring weekend here at school,' she wrote. 'I am sorry about the other weekend, and on the phone. If I come home next, please can we try not to argue. I know it's me, but I will try very hard, OK?' The bulk of her letter was concerned with some earrings she had purchased, a complaint about her father's failure to send a promised cheque and biscuits and half-hearted excuses for her bad marks in the recent exams.

'I do intend to get on better with you and the family from now on,' she concluded, 'but it's just 'cause I like my freedom . . . . When I'm seventeen I'll be able to get a flat with Nessie—if that's OK with you.'

Freedom! From what I wondered? What Vicky needed, or so it seemed to me, was freedom from herself and from all that drove her to make such misery, not only in the lives of others but also her own. Her attitudes of 'couldn't care less' didn't fool me. Her own father had admitted to me that he didn't dare to look into himself too closely because he feared what he might see. Only Jesus has the power to release us from those bonds—the fear of our own darkness, sin and condemnation. And so far neither Vicky—nor her father—wanted that kind of freedom.

In the meantime I sought help for her elsewhere. Having been told by a trusted Christian friend of a Spirit-filled psychiatrist who was in practice in a nearby town, I wrote, telling him the full story. Although unable to offer help himself since we were outside his area, and although he couldn't take on any private patients due to the pressure of work, he did give me hope.

'Perhaps in a way,' he wrote, 'you are really writing about your own problem, and it might therefore be more appropriate for me to see you . . . . May I suggest that the new Christian Counselling Service based locally may be able to help. I have some connection with the people there and would be able to give them supporting advice if they got into difficulty.'

Although I was never able to get Vicky to agree to talk to anyone else after her experience with Dr Sellick, I took up the suggestion that it might be appropriate for me to receive counselling, and benefited greatly during the next eighteen months in resolving some of my own conflicts. 'You can't be divorced from a difficult child as you can from a bad marriage,' I was reminded during that period. 'Perhaps the Lord is wanting to help you resolve this situation in a way that proved impossible with your ex-husband?'

Having finished her 'O' levels at boarding school, Sarah now began her sixth-form curriculum at the local comprehensive, despite the poor image given by my sister, Sally. We'd known from the start that there would be little choice at this stage, since the facilities for sixth-form work were almost non-existent at the convent, and neither would we have had the means to have all three girls at fee-paying schools. Ruth would be beginning her secondary education the following year, which would have meant a year's overlap.

For the intervening year, before Ruth started boarding, Vicky was to be the only one away—a fact which she reminded me of frequently.

'It's not fair,' she complained tearfully, week in and week out. 'I feel so out of things. You're all together during the week, and I don't feel one of the family when I come home.'

Eventually, by the end of the first term, I had been worn down to such an extent as to grant Vicky her wish. After a couple of interviews with the Heads of both schools, arrangements were made for her to leave the convent and spend her final two terms of schooling with Sarah in the local comprehensive. In retrospect, it may have been one of the worst mistakes I made. On the other hand, who is to say that Vicky would not have followed the same course of action at a later date had I kept her on at boarding school?

Freed from the strictures of convent life, it soon became apparent that she was completely beyond my control. Frequenting the pubs on a daily basis, she roamed the countryside with every undesirable within miles. Her new-found 'biker' friends, complete with leather gear, grimy hands and faces, earring-studded ears and noses, soon reduced her to their own level.

Gone was the cultured accent and modulated tone of voice which had been so widely praised and approved by my friends whenever Vicky had answered the telephone to them. The slovenly, grating intonation she adopted required some considerable effort on Vicky's part for some time, but eventually she mastered the technique of dropping 'h's and 't's as if she'd been born to it. Suffixing every phrase with a rising 'y'know?', her vocabulary diminished to a level of semi-literacy while blasphemous oaths became the order of the day.

'Why d'ya have to put on such a posh voice?' she scathingly asked me one day.

'It's just the natural way for me to talk,' I replied in bewilderment. 'I don't think about it.'

'You're just a snob,' she shouted on another occasion, banging down a milk bottle on the table so that it shot out all over the place. 'Why d'ya always put a milk jug out? Wot's wrong with the bo'le?'

She began wearing strange articles of clothing, all with an air of antiquity evidenced by the many holes, and all showing signs of that air of grey uniformity taken on by fabric which has long since forgotten the benefits of soap and water.

'Where did you get this from?' I would enquire, wrinkling my nose in disgust as I endeavoured to persuade her at least to have it washed.

'Oh, Python gave it to me,' she would reply casually. 'Python' was a friend unknown to me.

Needless to say, school work once more took a back

seat, so that at the end of her fifth-form year Vicky had little in the way of academic achievement and apparently less in the way of prospects. A polite letter from the Head informed me that she felt the comprehensive had nothing further to offer Vicky, and that due to her disruptive attitudes they felt it preferable that she should not contemplate another year at the school.

'I want to go in for hairdressing,' she begged me, her own unkempt mane defying the forces of gravity as it stood, nimbus like, around her head.

Metaphorically going down on bended knee, I pleaded her case at a nearby technical college, and despite her record and lack of the requisite number of 'O' levels, persuaded them to enrol her on a two-year course. This would give her a second chance at 'O' levels and CSE in maths, English, biology and French, as well as lessons in commerce, book-keeping and practical hairdressing.

'We aim to give our pupils the qualifications to start up their own salon,' I was told by the staff, to whom I'd had to give a sob-story of Vicky's broken home.

Since the college was too far from home for Vicky to commute daily, arrangements were made for her to board during the week at the college hostel. It seemed ironical that she had been breaking her neck to come home while at boarding school but was now so desperate to leave home once more. If nothing else, it at least gave me some respite from the daily confrontation of her steadily declining values.

Christmas came and went, and with it Vicky's first term at college. The second, too, passed relatively uneventfully. It was during the spring bank holidays that the tensions and aggressions of the last few years met in one mighty cataclysmic event.

As is so often the case, the actual incident which triggered off the clash is long since forgotten. The straw that breaks the camel's back is blown like chaff in the wind in the mighty force of the ensuing storm. Whatever it was, we were swiftly engaged in a fully-fledged battle of words and wills. A sense of impotence and despair, such as can only be known and understood by those who are themselves parents of wilful, delinquent or dissident teenagers, fanned the flames of my fury. I was shaking all over, my head throbbing and my heart racing, as streams of abuse flowed from the mouth of my daughter.

'I hate you.' Her long fair hair was a wild mane, partially obscuring her little round face. 'I'm not staying here to be treated like this. You've always hated me. I'm leaving home and never coming back.'

'Vicky,' my own voice was raised, my hand outstretched in an attitude of restraint.

'At least there's someone who cares for me,' her voice was hoarse with shouting, husky with emotion. 'I'll go and live with Toby when he gets out of prison. He'll have me.' Tears streamed from her eyes, streaking a blackened course down the still childish contours of her cheeks.

'And who is Toby?' I asked in alarm. 'You're still a minor, may I remind you.'

'He's a friend of mine. And he loves me. You don't know the meaning of the word.'

'Why is he in prison?' I shouted the question, intent on getting some answer from Vicky before she became any more hysterical.

'The police . . . . ' she spat the word out, her lip curling up contemptuously, 'took him in because he was on the beach when that girl got raped. Only she didn't. She made it up. Little bitch. She's nothing but a tramp. They'll have to let Toby go, then I'll live with him.'

'Rape? You're thinking of going to live with a rapist?' I blinked, a spell of dizziness coming over me.

'He's not!' Nearly beside herself, Vicky hurled the words at me in vitriolic profusion. 'He'll show me some love. You'll see. You never loved me. It was always Sarah this, Sarah that. Sarah, Sarah Sarah. That's all I've ever heard!'

Her face suffused with loathing, she turned to go.

Vainly I caught hold of her wrist, but breaking free of my grasp she ran from the house, stumbling blindly in an alcoholic haze, her hair streaming behind her.

For a moment I stood, transfixed. In the time it took me to collect myself and hurry up the path to the gate, she had disappeared. Breaking into a run, I raced to the end of the road. There was no sign of her. I had no idea which direction she had taken, nor whether she was on foot or with one of her biker friends. Fear gripped me, constricting my wildly thumping heart so that I felt a physical pain in my breast. Wearily I returned to the house. Where could I turn for help?

You can't just watch a sixteen-year-old walk out of your life and do nothing, but where do you go for advice? My parents were abroad on holiday. Several months into an interregnum, we had no vicar, and the church wardens, all well-respected members of our affluent community, would have no experience of such 'vulgar' behaviour I was sure. Somehow I doubted that they would even want to know. That left the doctor. Remembering how big a part our previous family doctor had played during my own childhood, before we'd moved south, that seemed to be the obvious answer. Seating myself at the telephone, I uttered a short prayer to the Lord, then dialled the surgery. It was my parents' GP to whom I'd turned for help, as we were now on his list since my confrontation with Dr Duffy. He had known me since my youth.

'I'm sorry, Meg,' the mellow tones came down the line. 'I couldn't possibly get involved. There's nothing I could really do. Why don't you ring Jim? He is her father, after all.'

I could hardly believe it.

Was I being old fashioned in supposing that a doctor might involve himself not only as a friend of the family, but also in viewing his patients as whole people whose health rested not simply in medical terms but in their emotional and spiritual well-being? Once again I felt betrayed; let down by the standards of care offered by modern medicine. I'd no wish to contact Jim at this juncture. He'd made clear his feelings regarding my abilities, and I had no desire to give him the opportunity to say, 'I told you so.' Nor, from several hundred miles' distance, was there much that he could accomplish. Besides, to turn to him before seeking the Lord on this matter would be tantamount to saying that Christianity didn't work.

'What do I do, Lord?' I asked, rubbing my hand across my throbbing forehead.

The social services—surely they would give me some help? There must be laws to protect children, and Vicky was still legally a minor. Feverishly I searched through the directory for the number. Nearly three quarters of an hour must have elapsed since Vicky had left. Memories of snippets read in newspapers crowded into my mind: heartbroken parents whose children had simply walked out of their lives, never to appear again; girls who were abducted, kidnapped, raped and murdered.

'Oh, Father, please protect her. Please look after her. Don't let anything happen to hurt her.'

She was on the water's edge, in his net. But did that mean she was really safe?

Connected at last to the social services, I blurted out my story.

'I'm awfully sorry . . . Mrs Scott did you say your name was?' The voice sounded like that of a young man, and though there was sympathy expressed in its tone, it was obvious that he, too, was about to offer cold comfort. 'Sixteen you said your daughter was? I'm afraid there's nothing we can do.'

'But surely . . . she's a minor. I thought children couldn't leave home without their parents' consent?'

'Technically no. Not if they can't support themselves.'

'Well she can't. She's no job, no savings.' Desperately I sought to persuade the owner of the suave tones to relent, to tell me he could help, to be my knight in shining armour riding to the rescue.

'That's true—to some extent.' Patiently he explained:

'You see, they can claim Supplementary Benefit at sixteen. So . . .' he paused, tutting empathetically. I could almost imagine him shrugging his shoulders in sympathy.

'So the government actually helps children who should be at home with their parents to be "self supporting" on the taxpayers' money?' I cried sarcastically. 'Vicky's never paid a penny to the Inland Revenue. Are you telling me that the tax I pay is used to help my child run away from home?'

'I am sorry Mrs Scott. Believe me, I do sympathize.'

'She's planning to go and live with an alleged rapist, you know,' I said abruptly. 'What does the state have to say about that?'

The young man sighed. 'Technically, Mrs Scott, a young person of sixteen is considered to be . . . "out of moral danger" is the term used. Once they pass that age, they're out of our jurisdiction. She can, therefore, live with whom she pleases.'

'Out of moral danger?' I echoed incredulously. 'But that's ridiculous. The law of the land says that a child under sixteen shouldn't have a sexual relationship. Why, suddenly, is it OK at sixteen to live with someone awaiting trial for rape?'

'I am sorry, Mrs Scott . . . .'

Thanking him for his trouble, I rang off. It wasn't his fault the law was such an ass. Frustration and rage now replaced my fear. What hope was there? All my life I'd believed that the British law was something to be proud of; something, if not infallible, at least secure and stable. Yet not only could the laws written into the statute books in a civilized and democratic country *not* be called on to aid one in the protection of young innocents, but other laws actually ran counter to them, undermining all that they stood for and actively opposing their enforcement! It seemed crazy to me.

A second phone call to the probationary service confirmed my thoughts. 'I'm afraid there's nothing we can do,' I was told, 'until after your daughter has got into trouble.' Sitting by the telephone in my little bucket chair, and gazing unseeingly out of the window to the cliffs beyond, I felt utterly bewildered.

'At least you used to know where you were with your children,' the mother of an errant young man had complained to me recently, when her son failed to turn up for an interview at the Home Office. 'Once upon a time, when they were financially dependent on you until they were twenty-one, you had some leverage. Now it seems anything goes.'

She'd had my sympathy when she'd recounted the story. Now, for the first time, she had my understanding. Parental authority had been eroded and usurped for years by successive governments. But we were not blameless—they'd been democratically elected by the populace. Society was now reaping the consequences of giving responsibility to youngsters too immature to know how to handle it. The 'right to freedom' advocated in our age had thus become a burden—a sheep in wolf's clothing. What greater right could a child have than to *be* a child?

Dusk was setting in when I was startled out of my reverie by the front door-bell. Switching on the sitting-room lamps, I rose and went to answer it, fear once more causing my heart to beat in staccato rhythm as I saw the blue-uniformed figure at the door. Had Vicky been found—a little battered body at the roadside, or stumbling blindly into a police station, the victim of a sex maniac?

'I just come up from the town, Mrs Scott,' the sergeant told me in a broad local dialect as I let him in. 'Your daughter was just coming out of the pub, and apart from the fact that she was high as a kite, and under age at that, she's gone off with what I can only term as un-desirables.'

'Oh, Mike, come on in.' Here at last was someone who cared enough to help. Why ever hadn't I thought of ring-ing the police earlier? Seated in the lamp-lit room, with the sergeant taking notes, I poured out the whole story.

'I know of this Toby you been talkin' 'bout,' he said in his slow way. 'It was the gang rape of a young girl of fifteen. Took place on a beach not far from here. I won't go into details, but there was seven or eight of them involved, and it weren't straight sex neither. Perversions such as I wouldn't mention to a lady. Enough said.'

'But what do I do, Mike? I've tried everyone I know and can't get any help. In any case, before she left Vicky said it was no good going after her, because even if I got her back, she'd run away again.'

'You gotta report it,' his gentle voice was so reassuringly firm. 'She's only a minor, see. An' if I were you, I'd have a word with the CID. Something's gotta be done to stop her. Mark my words, if she gets involved with that lot, she's really headin' for trouble.'

Promising to put in an official report registering Vicky's absence, the sergeant left. As soon as I'd closed the front door behind him, I returned to the lounge. Ruth was back at boarding school, her half-term having finished the previous week, and Sarah was away. I was therefore alone in the house. Dinner and other domestic details thus presented no problem, and seating myself once more beside the telephone, I dialled the CID in the city which was the administrative centre of the county. Nervous tension and exhaustion had set in, so that by the time the connection was made, I was having difficulty in controlling the tears which welled up in my eyes. The detective constable to whom I spoke could not have been more helpful, as he confirmed everything that our local bobby had told me and reiterated his warning.

'If something isn't done about your daughter pretty quick,' he forecast, 'I'd say that sooner or later we'll be picking her up. I hate to add to your worries, but the crowd she's running with are into drugs. If she's not involved already, it won't be long before she is.'

'But what can I do?' I asked in despair. 'I'm a single parent, her father lives in the North of England, and I just can't control her.' Swallowing hard, I struggled not to give in to the tide of emotion which threatened to engulf me. Already the tears were running freely down my face.

'The only course open to you is to make her a ward of court.' The gruff voice the other end had a kindly quality. This obviously wasn't the first time he'd handled a situation like this. 'Your local sergeant was quite right in advising you to report her running away,' he continued. 'If you don't, then you could be up for negligence. But in the long term, I think you need to take wardship proceedings. Otherwise you'll just be up against this time and time again, until she ends up in our hands.'

Thanking him for his help, I rang off, replacing the receiver with a loud clatter that rang through the empty room. Unable to restrain myself any longer, I gave way to my emotions, leaning my head and arms on the telephone table as I poured out a long stream of great gulping sobs.

7
Flight from Home

All that evening I sat by the phone, my muscles flexed in readiness to grab the receiver in the hope of hearing news of Vicky. None came. I could eat nothing, and it was only utter exhaustion which finally drove me to bed.
 ˙ Next morning, bleary eyed and thick headed, I faced the new day. It included an unalterable appointment at the bank.

'Don't let the phone ring while I'm out, Lord,' I prayed.

Sergeant Mike popped in, his cheerful florid face looking unusually grim. 'Any news?' he asked, dashing my hopes that he might have some for me.

The day stretched on interminably. I tried to immerse myself in some drawing and failed. Stretching the telephone flex to its extremities and carefully positioning it by an open window, I took myself off into the garden. Where creative pursuits fell short in enthralling my body and mind, keeping me from the tensions and fixations of fear, grubbing in the dirt was sure to succeed. 'One is nearer God's heart in a garden,' reads the old maxim, 'than anywhere else on earth.' While I could not altogether agree with its sentiments, I did find gardening a relaxation conducive to close communion with the Lord.

Even so, it was with considerable effort that I kept going. Numerous telephone calls to the local police station and the city-based CID had proved fruitless. Vicky, it seemed, had disappeared off the face of the earth. I'd felt it incumbent upon me to let Jim know after all, and had promised to contact him again as soon as I had news.

I was actually dozing before the fire late in the evening when the telephone rang. Its shrill tones had barely broken the silence before I shot from my chair. Fear rather than exertion made me breathless as I snatched the receiver to my ear.

'Yes?' Trembling, my heart thumping wildly, I waited apprehensively.

'Mrs Scott?' A male voice I did not recognize came down the line. 'This is the city police station, western division. We have your daughter in custody here.'

'In custody? What's she done?'

'You reported her missing, I believe?' Twisting the flex in one hand, I nodded foolishly in agreement. 'We picked her up a couple of hours ago outside a pub. There was some sort of brawl going on between herself and another girl. She's in quite a state, and we've had to lock her up to stop her running off.'

I sat down, shaking my head and feeling as if the stuffing had been knocked out of me.

'Are you still there, Mrs Scott? Can you come down to collect her?'

'Tonight?' It seemed ridiculous, but the thought of travelling all that way through open countryside to reach the city at this time of night filled me with horror.

'We can't keep her here, Mrs Scott. She's disturbing all the other inmates.'

It was the early hours of the morning by the time I found my way to the city police station, and there was a decided chill in the air. Wishing I'd taken time to put on something more substantial, I pulled my thin cardigan around my shoulders and walked into the austere-looking building.

'Like to have a word with you, please, Mrs Scott, before you see Vicky.' The constable on duty led me into a
small room, the bare brick walls of which had been
whitened in some sort of attempt to embellish it. Even
so, it had a cheerless atmosphere, augmented by the
single light bulb and utilitarian desk and chairs.

'She's quietened down a bit now,' he explained, seating himself opposite the chair he'd indicated for me to
take. 'Had some sort of family bust-up with her, did
you?'

I nodded agreement, too weary to go into lengthy
explanations.

'Well, Mrs Scott, the gist of it is this,' he spread his
large hands flat on the desk top and pursed his lips
beneath a large black moustache. 'Vicky's told us that if
you take her back home she'll only run away again
straight away. Said she'd climb out of the window if
necessary, and judging by what I've seen of her so far
this evening I wouldn't put it past her.'

'No,' I agreed, wondering what was coming.

He sighed deeply, then leaned back in his chair. 'What
I propose is this. Vicky's said she'll go and stay with a
chum from the tech. If you'll agree to that, and we know
where she is, then technically she won't have run away
from home.' He eyed me uneasily, evidently trying to
weigh up my reaction.

'You mean leave her here—in the city?' Drawing a
deep breath, I studied his grey eyes, unsure if I had
understood him correctly.

'That's right, Mrs Scott. You see as long as Vicky is on
our books as a missing person, we have to keep bringing
her in. If you take her home and she runs away again,
that means our men have to find her again—and again.'
He smiled encouragingly at me and turning sideways on
his chair, adopted a more relaxed pose, crossing one leg
over the other. 'If, however, you take her to this friend's
house and leave her there overnight, then that releases
us. She won't have run away, but will be there with your
consent.'

'Who is this friend?' I asked. 'And will she have her?'

'Oh yes, Mrs Scott.' Relief was written all over his face as he anticipated my agreement. 'She's a married lady. Well—divorced, I should say. Mind you, this would only be a temporary arrangement. I would most strongly advise you to make your daughter a ward of court.'

'That's what the CID man said,' I affirmed, a slight frown furrowing my brow.

'If you leave her with the sort of people she's been mixing with . . . well, she's heading for big trouble in my opinion. As a minor she's still your responsibility, and if you can't control her then it's up to you to find some other way.'

The late summer sun, glancing in sideways through the long sash window, pierced the shadow where it lay across Mr Fielder's desk. This was my third appointment with the tall thin solicitor, but I felt no more at ease with him than on first acquaintance. The news he had just given me made me feel decidedly apprehensive.

'Your daughter has filed an affidavit refuting many of your claims,' he said, his long slim hands opening up the file before him.

'Oh?' I squirmed uncomfortably in my chair. 'Could you be more specific?'

Mr Fielder donned a pair of spectacles which perched on the end of his nose as he read from the affidavit, summarising its contents. 'Victoria says that her friends are entirely suitable people; that the gentleman in prison was her boyfriend, but that she had no intention of living with him, and that it is not certain whether or not she will continue the relationship.'

What an unpleasant business this was turning out to be. On the advice of the police I'd gone ahead with the wardship proceedings, particularly after discovering that Vicky had been visiting her boyfriend in the county prison. A letter to the prison authorities had brought that to an end, once I'd explained that her interest was not entirely philanthropic, but that she herself was considered to be a prime candidate for their attentions.

Vicky had also informed me, somewhat belatedly, that she had resigned from the hairdressing course, and left the hostel to live with her college friend, Melanie. Mrs Pearce, the college tutor, had told me in confidence that Melanie was divorced with a child, and even now barely out of her teens was herself a subject of concern to the welfare department. 'She's a very nice girl,' she smiled, 'but she has a lot of problems and I would agree with the police that her home is hardly a suitable place for Vicky to live.'

There had been some question also about the men who frequented her home, and though, when I'd met her, Melanie seemed to be a very pleasant girl, I doubted that when the chips were down she would have any more success in dealing with Vicky's temper tantrums than I had.

Mr Fielder, the solicitor, cleared his throat. 'Victoria also says that she never had any desire to go on this course and that she is going to find work and attend night-school to improve her qualifications so that she can start another college course next year.'

'I had to beg to get her on that course,' I said, shaking my head in disbelief. 'That's what she said she wanted. And what will she do about a grant even if she does go on another course? As you know, my ex-husband has stopped paying all maintenance since going into voluntary liquidation.' I shrugged my shoulders, giving a small hollow laugh. 'And yet I'm being chased by the authorities to reimburse the grant and hostel fees still outstanding on the hairdressing course that Vicky's left.'

Mr Fielder shook his head in sympathy. 'There has also been a communication from the official solicitor suggesting that you, your daughter and the young lady with whom she is living should all try to get together with your ex-husband for a "round the table" talk,' he continued. 'It is his opinion, having met all concerned, that your fears concerning Victoria's well-being could be allayed if you could all talk together.'

Rubbing my hand over my brow, I closed my eyes

momentarily and sighed deeply. Mr Underhill, the official solicitor, had made perfectly clear his opinions when he'd met me. One could say that they were not dissimilar to those held by Dr Sellick, the child psychiatrist—namely that I held outmoded and unhealthy beliefs about the role of a parent in a child's life; that I sought to keep my daughter tied to my apron-strings, and, seemingly on the evidence that the Christian faith I professed had relevance to my whole way of life, it therefore followed that I must be somewhat fanatical.

I'd received so much conflicting advice prior to taking this action. Wardship proceedings had appeared rather extreme, yet if the police were to be believed—and they had been the only public sector who'd shown any positive concern—there had been little choice. Christian friends had not been so sure.

'Think of the prodigal son, Meg,' they advised. 'The father let his son go. Perhaps you should do likewise with Vicky.'

'If you do nothing and Vicky ruins her life, she'll always hold you responsible for not having taken action,' my mother and father countered. 'Parents have a duty to protect their children from self-destruction.'

In the end it had been prayer and the word of God which had decided me.

'Vicky is still a minor, and therefore your responsibility,' I seemed to hear the Lord telling me. 'I hold you accountable for her well-being until she is of age.' It seemed to me that the prodigal father had only let his son go when he came into his inheritance and was therefore no longer considered a minor (Luke 15:11–32).

This answer to prayer seemed to be reinforced through two subsequent Bible readings which I came across in my quiet times. The first was from Proverbs 13:24—'He who spares the rod hates his son, but he who loves him is careful to discipline him.' The second was the story of Eli's wicked sons, and the prophecy spoken against him and his household because he honoured them more than the Lord (1 Samuel 2:12–36). On all three counts, it had seemed to me that God was telling me that to trust him meant obeying his commands to be a responsible parent, even though that meant flying in the face of most of the advice around me.

Was it all worth it, I wondered? In the light of the battle I'd fought, standing out against the majority, I felt I might be forgiven for having my doubts. What had it actually achieved? Only further animosity between Vicky and myself, her father and myself, and my in-laws and myself. And yet despite my doubts, or more probably because of them, the Lord had reaffirmed my action. 'He will keep in perfect peace all those who trust in him, whose thoughts turn often to the Lord,' I read. (Isaiah 26:3, The Living Bible). Whatever happened, Vicky was still in his net on the water's edge.

Jim's bankruptcy and resultant cessation of maintenance had thrown me onto the social security, and, more importantly, into an even greater state of dependency and trust in the Lord than ever before. Our large and expensive house had, obviously, to be put on the market. It had, in any case, served its purpose of giving a measure of stability and security to the girls during the difficult months leading up to our divorce. But now, nearly four years on, it seemed to me that the Lord was leading me into a new thing.

The suggestion of a 'round-table' by the official solicitor had achieved little, to my mind, other than to illuminate the way in which the state sought to usurp parental authority in favour of children's 'rights'. In an effort to redress some sort of balance, I wrote the following February to the official solicitor, pointing out how I saw a child's 'rights', in what I believe to be a biblical view:

> My love for her is in the realms of care and concern, in wanting what is best for Vicky. I cannot reconcile what Vicky wants as always being what is best for her. She is still a child and as such has the right to expect such love and concern from me and a sense of responsibility from those concerned in her welfare. The law in its wisdom(?) sees fit to thrust such responsibility upon youngsters before they are

able to cope with it, relinquishing adult responsibility in so doing.

It transpired that Vicky had fallen out with Melanie, and expressed a desire to live alone, to which suggestion the official solicitor gave his blessing. My letter concluded by asking whether he would want his daughter, if he had one, to live alone in similar circumstances.

It seemed to me that the parents whom the law undermines are the very ones who are left to pick up the pieces when it all backfires on children who are unable to cope with the call for self-discipline and maturity thrust upon them. Surely a child's greatest 'right'—and a God-given one at that—is to be a child?

A visit to Vicky's new abode in the early spring seemed to confirm my worst fears. The filth and squalor was beyond description, and I was horrified that I had taken Ruth to witness the depths to which her older sister had sunk. The foul smell of rotting food and unwashed bodies hung in the air, while a black, greasy grime rendered all the meagre furnishings a colourless, uniform grey. The walls had been painted some lurid shade of purple. In one corner of the room a snake, in a glass tank, was fed live mice by one of Vicky's companions. Overflowing ash-trays, had evidently been supplemented by dirty coffee mugs, so that the stub-ends of cigarettes formed a noxious, glutinous mess in the dregs of liquid.

'Would you like a cup of coffee?' Vicky asked.

Tears started to my eyes as, unable to bring myself to take a seat, let alone put anything to my lips, I shook my head. She herself had the same general air of grime and slovenliness about her, her hair matted, her clothes dejected. How could any human being be reduced to such a level? Who but Satan could conspire to debase God's creation, made in his image, to such depths?

Stumbling blindly from the flat, Ruth and I took our leave. Struggling to check the tears which now flowed freely down my face as I drove home, I tried to comfort Ruth who sobbed quietly in the back of the car.

8

Bad Company

'Well—there's our new home town.'

Turning briefly to Ruth, I changed down a gear and began the long descent to the city which was spread before us. The river, winding its way seaward, shone in the late summer sun like a blue satin ribbon woven into the countryside. A sudden thrill of excitement shot through me as I surveyed it all, lifting the vague sense of depression and uncertainty which had enveloped and silenced us both since leaving home.

Only it wasn't home any more. The removal van was, even now, on its way to our new address, and the house which had been meant to give such a wonderful new start to Jim and me nearly ten years ago was in the possession of strangers.

I'd kept it on deliberately after our divorce, battling against all odds, determined to give the children some sort of security. Damp, neglect, lack of finance for repairs, and still less energy for the steadily encroaching army of weeds in the garden had all eventually won the day. Jim and I had lived apart for nearly five years now, and when he'd suddenly stopped paying maintenance two years previously, it had been only a matter of time before losing the house.

It wasn't a good time for selling, but to begin with I

hadn't minded. It had given Sarah an opportunity to finish her schooling and to start her subsequent college course. Latterly, however, it had been a real struggle as I'd juggled Supplementary Benefit payments with a part-time office job and bed-and-breakfast guests in the season. Unable to cope with the sudden downward trend in our financial standing, Sarah had moved out, finding digs in the nearby town more conducive to studying during the last terms of her further education.

Outwardly, any sign of insecurity in her demeanour would have been hard to detect, but as her mother I was well aware of the effect recent events had had upon her. To lose your father to another family was bad enough, but the sudden crash of Jim's business and its effect on the material trappings of our affluent life, as well as the consequent loss of face with her peer group, had seemed to be the final straw.

It had hurt, watching the steady decline in the spiritual and emotional stability in this, my eldest daughter. 'Why don't you go to Hildenborough Hall?' I'd suggested on numerous occasions, having myself benefited enormously from the Christian ministry, teaching and fellowship at the centre. 'It's really super there. I'm sure you'd enjoy it, especially if you went for one of the Young People's Weekends.'

Like many teenagers, she'd dug in her heels, refusing to take the counsel of her mother. Eventually I'd kept quiet, resorting to prayer and the intervention of the Lord to sort her out. When a decent length of time had elapsed, she'd announced her intention of going to Hildenborough, just as if I'd never mentioned it before and the idea had been all her own.

I was delighted. Sarah had made a commitment to the Lord about ten years previously, when she'd been only nine years old. I had no doubt as to its reality, but the events of the last few years had taken their toll. If she found a new depth of faith and trust in God, as I hoped she would, then the experiences she'd undergone could be used by him in the accomplishing of his promise that 'all things work together for good' for those who love him (Romans 8:28, Authorized Version).

And that was what happened. She returned home radiant, her love for the Lord on fire, and with a whole new circle of friends.

'They've invited me up next weekend,' she said, her eyes shining hopefully. 'You don't mind do you?'

Little realizing what this was to mean, I'd readily given my blessing. The Lord was obviously doing a new thing in her life.

'Mummy,' she'd shrieked excitedly down the telephone when she'd called home, 'You'll never guess what! They persuaded me to apply for a job with a Christian firm advertised in *Buzz*. It's in the West End— and I've been accepted! I start next month—I told them I hadn't even finished my personal assistant's course, but they didn't seem to mind. Just think— London!'

I was thinking! At least as well as my reeling mind would allow. It would have pleased me better had she moved with us and found a job locally, but I soon realized that having entrusted her to the Lord, he obviously had other plans.

Of Vicky we'd seen little, I'd arranged meetings with her on two or three occasions in the town in which she was living, but had never again been able to steel myself to visit her flat. The depths to which she'd sunk had so appalled me, it was beyond my capabilities to face it again.

She'd been hard and unyielding with me as we'd sat over coffee in one of the department stores, and though polite, had given me to understand that she would never fully forgive me for the action I'd taken. Be that as it may, I'd been at pains to affirm my continuing love for her, though other than simply telling her, and giving her the odd bit of cash, she made any demonstration of affection well nigh impossible, spurning any physical touch whatever. Perhaps now, with the prospect of our new home in a new environment, far from the memories of previous bad times, some bridges could be built. Surely curiosity, if nothing else, would prevail upon her to seek us out?

Sure enough, within two months of our move, Vicky was suggesting a visit.

'Could you pick me up?' she asked on the telephone. 'I'm sorry, Mum, but I don't know exactly where you are.'

'Of course I will,' I cried delightedly. Our house was on the outskirts of the city, and though I knew that Vicky hitch-hiked everywhere—much against my will— and seemed to have little problem in finding her way all round the country, even travelling north to visit her father when the mood took her, I was glad of this rare opportunity to be able to do something for her.

'Where shall I meet you, love?'

'Oh—by the bus station,' she replied. 'I know where that is.'

She looked unwell, I thought, as I drew into the bus depot next day. Grey-faced and thin, there was a general air of neglect about her. I'd never really got used to the ragged clothes she wore, though true to form, she was hardly in the car before boasting about her latest purchase.

'Ten pence at the Oxfam shop.' Proudly she held out some barely recognizable garment for my inspection. 'Good innit?' she continued brightly.

Taking advantage of her good mood, I reached forwards and pecked her on the cheek—quickly, before she could recoil.

'Toby's going to be out on parole soon.'

It was difficult to keep up with the bright banter and sudden changes of subject. 'She's probably trying to make friends again with me,' I thought. Trying—and trying too hard. It was all rather forced, but I felt sorry for her and wanted to help in her clumsy attempts at reconciliation.

'Oh?' Carefully keeping my eyes on the road as I negotiated the traffic on the way home, I kept my voice as light and casual as possible 'Have you seen him then?'

'Yeah. Just been in this morning.'

Was there a note of defiance? She was eighteen now. Was she demonstrating to me that for all the strictures I'd placed on her visiting the prison in the past, there was nothing I could do now? Nodding in what I hoped was a non-committal fashion, I deftly changed the subject, pointing out the sights of my new home town.

It didn't take long to show Vicky around our new house when we got home. It was nothing like the size of the last, and with that topic exhausted, conversation took a decided downward trend thereafter. It was difficult to know which subjects were not taboo; the past was too painful, and we seemed to have little in common at present. Even when Ruth returned home from school, Vicky kept up an air of bright banality. The whole tenor of our relationship was reminiscent of fencing partners, making little probing thrusts and parries as we verbally skirted cautiously around each other. Before we went to bed there was talk of Vicky leaving first thing in the morning.

'I have to get back to sign on,' she excused herself, lighting the umpteenth cigarette.

'But you've hardly been here two minutes.' It was out before I could stop myself and, kicking myself inwardly, I sensed her bristling at this attempt to pin her down.

'I never said I'd be staying long,' she said hotly, jumping up from her chair and inhaling deeply. 'I shan't get my Giro if I don't sign on.'

In the event, despite my half-hearted attempt to persuade her otherwise, it was with some relief that I saw her off in the morning. Things had been so strained between us all. The distant politeness could not have lasted. Sooner or later the tensions lurking beneath the surface would have burst through the thin skin of superficiality. I was tired, too, having been awake all night as Vicky had prowled the house, smoking and making innumerable cups of coffee throughout the early hours. It would obviously take more than the odd visit to sort out our relationship problems.

Some sort of order was beginning to emerge from the chaos of our move, and thoughts of how I should earn a living were now taking precedence in my mind, though I planned to leave the reality of such consideration until after Christmas. Ruth and I had settled on a house church as our new fellowship. With an abundance of love and understanding we had been welcomed and accepted in a way which was quite overwhelming. And with weekly house-groups, where everyone was committed to the spiritual and practical welfare of the others, we had quickly made friends.

Vicky had once more disappeared from the scene having satisfied her curiosity about our new abode, and though she was never far from my mind, the news which I received a few weeks after her visit came like a bolt from the blue.

Winter mists and the damp raw cold of November kept me huddled close to the fire in the evenings, so it was with some reluctance that I was dragged away by the ringing of the telephone.

'Meggie? It's me.' Jim's voice was clipped, but I wasn't surprised. He'd put up so much opposition at our last meeting over Vicky's wardship, and had made perfectly clear his feelings about my action. All that surprised me was that he should phone at all.

'Is anything wrong?' I asked threading the telephone through the banisters and seating myself half way up the stairs so as to be out of earshot of Ruth.

'The police have just rung me. They've taken Vicky into custody.' Starkly, brutally, the news was given.

'Where? When? What's happened?'

Despite the shock, my mind was already pondering the question as to why they had rung Jim and not me. Vicky had, after all, been in my custody prior to her reaching the age of majority, and in any case Jim lived hundreds of miles away.

'Drugs!'

Did I detect a hint, in Jim's laconic tones, suggestive of

a struggle with his emotions? Whatever his sentiments, the word hit me between the eyes so that for a moment the world around me seemed to reel.

'Drugs?' I gasped. 'How?'

'I'm sorry, Meggie. I seem to have made such a mess of everyone's life.' Jim's voice came miserably down the line. 'She hasn't actually been taking them as far as the police can tell. Seems she just helped herself to a box of drugs from the back of a lorry delivering to a chemist shop.'

'But whatever for?' Feelings of dizziness and an air of unreality swept over me. Leaning forwards on the step, I rested my head on my knees, still gripping the telephone receiver tightly in my now clammy hand.

'She was with some other yobs. But she won't say who.'

'Oh, Jim . . . .' My voice broke. 'What's going to happen? Can I speak to the police direct?'

'I shouldn't bother,' Jim seemed to have control of himself once more. 'They spoke to Sheila earlier, when I was out, and said they'd ring back if there was any further news.'

My head shot up. They'd spoken to Sheila? On what grounds did they speak to her? I was Vicky's mother. It was on the suggestion of the police that I'd brought the wardship case in the first place. Why, now, was I being ignored.

'Thanks for letting me know. You'll ring if there's any further news?' I asked Jim coldly.

'Yes, of course. And you the same.'

It was difficult to know which emotion was uppermost as I replaced the receiver. Concern and fear for Vicky's safety fought with anger and hurt pride that Sheila had been informed of my daughter's plight.

'Forgive me, Lord,' I leaned my head on my knees once more, the tears starting to my eyes. 'Feeling jealous of Sheila isn't really appropriate at present, but I do Lord. Did Jim talk the police into believing that they would be better not dealing with me? Why, Father, Why?'

'What's the matter, Mummy?' Ruth opened the lounge door and peered up at me through the banisters.

'Nothing, darling.' Brushing my hands across my eyes to remove all trace of tears, I answered brightly, reassuringly. 'I've just got to make another phone call. You go back in the warm. I'll be in soon.'

It was unfortunate that this news should come at the weekend when Ruth was at home. Though fourteen years of age by now, she was still showing considerable signs of stress since our divorce, and was very immature for her age. I'd kept her on at boarding-school for this first term so that she wouldn't have to cope with the trauma of a new school at the same time as a new home and new town, but it couldn't last. There were no more funds available for the fees, and in any case she'd begged to be allowed to go to a day-school. Whatever else happened, I had to do my best to protect her from this latest upheaval. Sighing deeply, I reached for the phone and began to dial the police station.

It was a chilly but sunny December morning when Vicky was set to appear before the magistrates' court in the town in which she lived. My telephone calls to the police had proved fruitless, except in so far as I had registered the fact that I, not Sheila, was Vicky's mother.

'I'm very sorry, Mrs Scott,' the sergeant had apologized. 'I was led to understand that the other lady was Victoria's mother. I'm afraid I didn't even know of your existence.'

It hurt to know that either Jim, or Mr Underhill, the official solicitor, had deliberately made sure that all enquiries were addressed to Jim's home in the north, rather than mine only a few miles distant. Moreover Sheila herself must have allowed the sergeant to assume that she was Vicky's mother, and made no reference to my existence.

'It really makes you feel you've been cast off like an old shoe,' I told my mother. She and my father had insisted on giving up their time in order to accompany me to the court. 'You'll need some support,' they said kindly, 'especially if Jim turns up with Sheila.'

I had to admit, as I turned into the carpark to meet them prior to the hearing, I was glad of their insistence. My knees were trembling as we went into the court, and it was good, at least, to have someone to talk to.

I knew, too, that those few Christians with whom I'd shared the story, would all be praying for the outcome. Everybody in my house-group had been wonderfully supportive. Even so, admitting that your daughter is associated with people involved in crime of this magnitude—rape and drugs—is hardly something to be broadcast far and wide. There were feelings of loyalty too. Vicky was my daughter, and I loved her. Real love 'always protects, always trusts, always hopes, always perseveres. (1 Corinthians 13:7) How could I expose Vicky's problems to relative strangers who couldn't possibly feel as I did towards her?

The hearing revealed little which was new to me. Only Vicky's appearance and demeanour were to shock me that morning, Her hair, a tangled mane as always, had been dyed a vivid Titian hue. Black kohl ringed her eyes, while her mouth was a slash of scarlet. Always slim and petite, her figure left nothing to the imagination, etched, as it was, in a pair of skin-tight black ski-pants now showing a brown tinge of age.

Her eyes roved the court as she nodded in our direction, smiling over-brightly. Jim was conspicuous by his absence on this occasion, and it was obvious that Vicky had expected him to be there. Still she had refused, to the last, to reveal the names of her accomplices, and I sensed in the magistrates something of that same frustration which had filled me when dealing with the child of yesteryear. A general air of cocky and perverted pleasure seemed evident in the replies she made, and I wept inwardly to see the outworking of so low a self-esteem that it had to resort to this for attention.

'Why did you take this case of drugs, Scott?' the magistrate asked, once the preliminaries were taken care of.

'I just saw it there,' Vicky's head came up defiantly.

'You just saw it there?'

'Yeah.'

'Did you have any purpose in taking those particular drugs?'

'Nope.'

'So why did you take them?'

'Just seemed like a good lark. The van was open, an' I saw it there.' Vicky looked around the court as a schoolgirl, caught in some prank, might seek the approval of her classmates.

It was all over so quickly. Probation was arranged, pending a county court appearance, with Vicky now required to report on a weekly basis to the official solicitor because of her recent involvement with him. A few moments for headshaking; hurried, strained sentences passing between mother and daughter; then out into the sunshine.

'I'm off now,' Vicky said in passing.

'Why don't the two of you have a coffee together in town,' my father suggested quietly, drawing me aside. My heart sank at the thought of having to make conversation. What was there to say? But I obediently put the proposal to Vicky and, to my surprise, she accepted.

'I see Dad didn't bother to turn up,' she said bitterly as we sipped our hot drinks and thawed in the warmth of the busy little café.

'He probably had an important business engagement,' I replied.

It seemed doubtful to me. What could be more important than your daughter? Still, it wouldn't help to voice my true thoughts in that respect.

'I might spend a few days with him,' Vicky went on. 'He did suggest it a while back.'

'Good idea,' I said, then thought, 'Strange how strong the blood-tie can be. Children are like dogs—even if you kick them, they keep coming back.'

'What about Christmas?' I asked lightly. 'Will you be home?'

She shrugged, pursing the scarlet slash, now smudged

and muted where it had been deposited against the side of the cup. 'Perhaps,' she said. 'We'll see.'

It was to be the first of several Christmases without her. Even though I'd known, inwardly, that her presence would have put tremendous strains and tensions on the family, it was strange to be so depleted, and my heart was heavy at the realization of what was happening to us all. I had only once spent Christmas away from my family, and that had been because of a spell in hospital. It was inconceivable to my parents and sisters that we should not all be together. Was this a herald of the disintegration of that dream?

It had taken some weeks for a date for Vicky's county court appearance to be set, and in the meantime I had found a job. It was embarrassing, having to explain within days of starting, that I should need time off to attend, but my boss had been most kind and understanding as I'd made a clean breast of it all. I'd been assured, too, of plenty of prayer support by my housegroup in whom I'd also confided. And as it had happened, it had not been too bad.

Vicky had been put on probation, so that in effect the official solicitor was once more her guardian and mentor, with the weekly reporting order to continue for a further year. Inevitably, Ruth had had to be told something, as had Sarah. Vicky's absence at Christmas-time, the constant telephone calls, and the strained expression which I knew was evident on my face could not be hidden indefinitely. I kept it minimal, intent on preserving some semblance of reputation for Vicky, as well as protecting her sisters from further anxiety.

Barely a month later, just as life had begun to settle down once more, there was further news of Vicky, and the whole merry-go-round began again.

'Sorry to 'ave to tell you, Mrs Scott,' the familiar accents of Sergeant Mike came down the wire, 'but we 'ave Vicky in custody.'

My heart sank. It seemed inconceivable that she should once more have got into trouble, especially so soon after the last.

'It won't go well for her in court,' Jim said when I telephoned him. 'What a little fool!'

'You don't think she's doing it to get attention, do you?' I asked.

'Well, she's certainly succeeding,' he replied angrily.

I was glad my parents had once more given me their support in accompanying me to the court. The wind whipped stingingly across my face as I approached the entrance, head down and pulling my coat collar higher. Only as I passed through the revolving doors and lifted my eyes did I realize that Sheila, too, had accompanied Jim. My heart lurched. Though the Lord had dealt with me in the realms of my forgiveness of her, it was a traumatic experience having to come into contact with the woman who had destroyed your marriage. Somehow it seemed even more difficult that she had at one time been a friend. What did one say? Was there a protocol to deal with so strange a set of circumstances?

'Are you Vicky's parents?' a begowned and bewigged court official asked of no one in particular.

'Yes,' Jim replied.

'Would you like to come this way then please,' He strode off, including Sheila in his conversation, leaving me to trail along behind. I felt windswept and bedraggled in comparison to Sheila's neat appearance, having had no time to go to the ladies' room.

We were led into a small room and seated around a large table which almost filled its dimensions.

'Now,' the official donned a pair of half-spectacles and peered at an untidy sheaf of papers which he clutched in one hand. He had an air of busyness and haste about him, exacerbated by a great celerity of speech. 'The official solicitor has made representation to us on your daughter's behalf, and it has been felt that if some agreement could be made prior to the hearing as to a probation recommendation, His Honour, Judge Sykes, might look upon that as a favourable alternative to a term of punitive measures.'

'You mean if arrangements can be made for Vicky to live with one of us, she won't have to go to prison?' Jim's quick mind made what I guessed was a fairly accurate interpretation of the legal jargon.

'Precisely.' He beamed at Jim before consulting his papers once more. 'I believe that you have already discussed this with the official solicitor? Mrs Scott?' Sheila and Jim nodded an affirmative, though with some embarrassment I fancied. Was this a cooked-up job between the three of them? I cleared my throat.

'That is, as long as my ex-wife is in agreement,' Jim's conscience must have been working overtime. 'How do you feel, Meggie,' he asked, turning to me, 'if a suggestion is put forward for Vicky to come and live with us?'

Thoughts of all I had fought against down through the years crowded into my mind: the children being brought up to drink alcohol, to have worldly attitudes, and low standards of morality. I thought of how weakly I'd given in at every stage so that my fight had been mere empty words. Nor, in recent years, had my own life been exemplary.

'Give me wisdom now, Lord, please.' I prayed silently. I'm so tired of all the battles. I just don't think I've the strength to cope with Vicky any more, plus living alone, trying to earn my keep, and give Ruth back some sort of stability.'.

'Ruth has been showing signs of nervous strain for some years now, as you know,' I said aloud. 'Changing her home, home town and schools has been a tremendous upheaval for her, and she's finding it extremely difficult to settle in and make new friends.' I looked downwards, gripping my hands tightly together in my lap. With a sudden flash of self-awareness, I realized just how exhausted I felt, how near to breaking-point.

'I don't think it would be fair on her to have Vicky around, with all the attendant worry and rows, just when she's starting her 'O' level curriculum for real,' I said resignedly, looking round the table. 'But I am Vicky's mother, and I do love her. I would like that point to be made. If she goes to her father it would be because I believe that to be the best for all concerned, not because I can't be bothered with her.' It was a long speech and I felt breathless and embarrassed, aware that my cheeks felt hot.

It seemed to me that had Jim not taken my opinions into account, there would have been no reference to my feelings whatever. As it was, the matter was arranged as well as it could be before the hearing, and within moments we were summoned to the courtroom.

There must have been eight or ten of them involved, all with the appearance of being the dregs of society, though to my surprise some had the cultured tones and educated speech of affluent home backgrounds. All were accused of breaking into and entering a health centre and of stealing drugs from the premises. Vicky had acted as lookout, but the full significance of her part was only later to hit me. The gang had travelled a considerable distance from their own city centre to a small and remote village in order to undertake their criminal activity. Only Vicky could have known the layout of that particular surgery, and only she the extent of embarrassment caused. It was none other than the place where we had lived for the past ten years, and where her grandparents still lived. Was she trying to hit where it hurt most?

At last it was over, and despite the gravity of this second brush with the law and the fact of her being on probation already, Vicky was given a suspended sentence. The recommendations of the official solicitor, through the official we had spoken to, having been put to the Judge, a two-year probationary period was settled on, to be spent in the home of her father.

'Well, at least she's not being sent to prison,' my father said, taking my arm to lead me out. 'Though sometimes I think a short sharp shock might do her more good than any two-year probation.'

'It's difficult to know,' I sighed. 'People tell me that being brought into such close proximity with convicted

criminals has an inuring effect and makes them more
hardened still.'

'Well, it won't do Jim any harm to see just what you've
been up against and to take a bit more responsibility
with her,' my mother said. 'It's all too easy condemning
you for the wardship proceedings without actually having any personal knowledge of how difficult Vicky is.'

'Don't worry, Mrs Scott,' the slovenly and slurred
speech of one of the gang assailed my ears as we left the
court. 'Vicks ain't s'bad. She's a real doll reely. We'll look
after 'er for ya.'

I could feel myself recoiling as the youth lurched towards me. Dressed in baggy, calf-length trousers made
of striped pillow ticking, he had a shiny, shaven head, at
variance with the stubble on his chin and lip. One ear
was punctuated with rings and studs, and an assortment
of safety-pins and zips adorned his person.

'How dare he talk to me about my daughter,' I
thought. 'Who does he think he is to attempt to reassure
me?'

Struggling inwardly to regain my composure, I
turned my back and walked away. 'Jesus died for him.'
The thoughts crowded in. 'God loves that . . . that crea-
ture . . . as much as he loves me. How can he when he's
so detestable?'

A hand touched my arm. Whirling in expectation of
confronting the skinhead once more, I found Mr
Underhill, the official solicitor, at my side.

'Perhaps it might have been better if Vicky's wardship
had gone through earlier,' he said. 'I'd no idea she was
into this. I'm sorry, Mrs Scott.'

With obvious embarrassment he scurried away, losing
himself quickly among the crowd as I stared thoughtfully after him.

9

A Twilight World

I was glad, as I drove home later, that there was now someone in my life with whom I could share the torrent of feelings within. Peter and I had met some months previously, through other Christians, and had found we had much in common. The Lord had given me a great burden for those who had suffered broken marriages, and increasingly I found myself involved in counselling in this and other areas. It transpired as we shared that Peter, a bachelor himself, also had a great concern for the lonely. Within a short time of our meeting, we found ourselves launching forth into a ministry together, setting up and leading a self-help group for Christian singles.

Tall, with kindly grey eyes, Peter had all the qualities of patience and gentleness that had for so long been lacking in my life. Gradually, as friendship had developed into love, he'd proved an invaluable support in the traumas I'd been experiencing with Vicky. God is good! He'd provided, at exactly the right moment, the man whose steady, prayerful concern was to be such an influence in my life in the future.

But in the meantime God had much to teach me in spiritual matters, particularly in the realms of inner healing. We had all suffered greatly during the years leading up to the final breakdown of my first marriage, and the children, no less than I, were left with emotional wounds which profoundly affected our whole outlook on life. Surrounded by the love of our house-church fellowship, Ruth and I were gradually enabled to unwind from the tensions and strains of recent events.

For myself, that learning meant making discoveries, under the guidance of the Holy Spirit, which stretched back many years into my past life. As the New Year unfolded into spring, I found myself embarked upon a course of reading material which was to reveal much of the cause and effect of my attidudes and behaviour, and I was able to understand for perhaps the first time my own culpability in the relationship problems of my marriage.

The Lord seemed to lead me, without any outside intervention, to reading matter which opened up hitherto unknown areas. It was as if the Holy Spirit turned a spotlight on all the dark and hidden corners within, revealing old wounds inflicted on me since earliest childhood, innocently or otherwise, by parents, siblings, teachers, and friends. And as I was led to repentance for my attitudes and forgiveness for those who had wronged me, so gradually I was released into the freedom won for me by Christ.

If this was possible for me, I soon realized, then it must also be possible for my children. And so I began to pray that the Holy Spirit would take me back into the past and show me any and all harm I might have inflicted on the girls as a result of bad parenting, selfishness, thoughtlessness, mistaken judgements and omission. Over a period of weeks I worked systematically on everything he revealed, asking forgiveness—even for those things I had imposed on them in ignorance or fear—and 'loosing' them to the Lord (Matthew 18:18). I also prayed for their healing, and asked that even the things that others had inflicted on them might have no permanently harmful effect.

Vicky in the meantime, according to the probation

order laid down by the court, had been living with her
father in the north. It was therefore with some surprise
that I learned, some months later, that she had left his
home and made her way to London.

'I can't understand it,' I told my parents, shaking my
head in disbelief. 'Jim just seems to accept it and is making no attempt to get her back or enforce the order.'

'I should have thought it was tantamount to contempt
of court,' my father said. 'And London is hardly the best
place for her to be. Why ever doesn't he take a more
responsible role with her?'

'Well,' I shrugged my shoulders, raising my eyebrows
and pursing my lips, 'there's not much I can do. I don't
know where she's living or who her probation officer is.'

It worried me, nevertheless, but strangely, not as
much as my parents. They did not share my faith, and
had therefore no way of grasping the vision which the
Lord had given me.

'I know that ultimately Vicky will be in the palm of
God's hand,' I confided in a Christian friend, 'but even
so—I am afraid of what might befall her in London
before that time.'

One afternoon, soon after her departure from her
father's home, Vicky telephoned to say that she was in
the area and would like to see me. Still no more used
than I had ever been to her unkempt appearance, I was
as shocked as ever to see her grey little face peering out
from under the wild mane of hair. A diamond stud
through one nostril and a row of earrings up one ear did
nothing to allay my fears as to her lifestyle. To me they
were like signposts or advertisements, pointing to a life
quite alien to all that I had hoped for her.

'How are things?' I asked, setting two coffees on the
table as we settled ourselves in the lounge. Conversation
with her was like walking on eggshells. The least wrong
move on my part would, I knew, utterly crush all hope
of communication.

'I expect you heard about Dad and me?' Her face
hardened as she threw herself down on the settee.

'He said you'd moved out.' Tentatively I sipped at the hot liquid.

'I suppose he told you I'd been drinking?'

Forcing myself to relax, I leaned back in my chair. 'He just said there'd been a row.'

She'd been like a caged lion since her arrival, but my statement seemed suddenly to release the pent-up nervous energy, galvanizing Vicky into violent reaction. Leaping from the settee, she exploded.

'I had been drinking, but so had he and Sheila. They spend half their time p***** out of their minds.'

'Vicky!' I could not let such language go unremarked.

'Oh, sorry Mum.' She grinned sheepishly before resuming her tirade. 'Anyway, Dad ordered me back into the house. Said he'd lock me in my room. When I shouted back at him, he grabbed me by the hair and dragged me out of the car and across the road.'

Obviously not satisfied with my carefully concealed reaction to this news, she lifted her skirt to reveal deep grazes the length of one thigh.

'Look!' she burst out contemptuously. 'He dragged me even after I fell. He was drunk and so was Sheila. She was shouting at him, and he was shouting at me and I was just crying. I'm not going back there to be treated like that.'

I could imagine the scene only too vividly. Jim had always been a hardened drinker, and my heart went out to Vicky. It was not the first time drink had been responsible for scenes of violence in our family. Still, I also knew how Vicky could inflame you, winding you up until you were on the verge of losing control. 'It'll do Jim good to have to deal with it for once,' I thought. 'But by the sound of it, once had been enough. No wonder he wasn't anxious to have Vicky back again!'

'Mum, I shall have to go. I told Melanie I'd be down to see her this afternoon. Half my clothes are at her house and I need them for London. She'll wonder where I am if I don't get there soon. Anyway, I want to see the new baby. She's so cute. You should see her . . . .'

Rambling on, Vicky took her leave. She'd visited for barely half an hour, but it was obvious that she was racked with cravings and needs which prohibited her remaining any longer. Remembering how restless I had been during my days of smoking, there was an odd experience of identification within me for her dilemma. The yearnings of nicotine addiction had left me unable to settle in the presence of my parents' disapproval, and I guessed Vicky had a similar problem with me, despite my avowed acceptance of the fact that she smoked.

Nevertheless, I wept inwardly as I waved goodbye. It seemed such a waste of her young life. She had come from pain and unhappiness, and seemed to be going nowhere to alleviate her distress. The pleasure-seeking of her father as a means of anaesthetizing himself against all he sought to escape was one thing, but his way, though equally potentially destructive, was at least socially acceptable. Jim worked hard and played hard, and while over-indulgence in the three great aims of the world—wine, women and song—abused God's laws of creation and therefore physical and mental health, they were at least brought into being by the sweat of his brow.

Vicky's way of life was different. Utterly dependent on social security, she lived in such a way as not only to abuse her own health, but also as an affront to decent, law-abiding citizens. And while it could be argued that she had much against her during her nineteen years, there could be no doubt, either, that she had enjoyed material benefit and loving care denied the vast majority of this world.

A telephone call from Jim, some time after Vicky's visit, shed further light on the drunken brawl which had taken place outside his home. He had in fact rung on another matter, but inevitably Vicky's name had cropped up as he asked if I had seen her.

'I suppose she told you some cock-and-bull story?' he enquired tentatively.

'She said there had been a row,' I replied cautiously.

'Too right there was! I don't suppose she bothered to

elucidate? She'd been receiving mail from the blokes in prison. You may not approve, but I've been steaming it open.' He coughed—a habitual sign of embarrassment. 'Just wanted to know what she's up to. Some of the things written in those letters shocked even me. Stupid little fool! She's still infatuated by this fellow she was going out with.'

'So what happened?' I asked sympathetically.

'We had a blazing row. I said I'd lock her in her room. No doubt you know the rest.'

It was difficult to sort out the rights and wrongs. Having been on the receiving end myself from both parties, my feelings were mixed. They were so alike, Jim and Vicky. Each seemed to bring out the worst in the other, but that was not the whole story. I knew from personal experience years ago that excesses of alcohol could change one's whole personality. Perhaps it was not change but suppression; suppression of whatever is decent and moral in man so that the 'natural' man is given full rein. It was a frightening thought.

By late spring the same year, after much prayer and heart-searching, Peter and I decided to get engaged. Our romance had developed into a relationship of mutual love and esteem, yet it was a momentous decision and required a good deal of courage on both our parts.

It was quite a thought for me, to go back into a state of commitment to a man after the failure of the last. For the past six or seven years I had lived in a position of paradox, whereby I had both longed to love and be loved, to have and to hold, to be cherished and cared for, and yet had enjoyed a measure of independence never before known to me, and had feared its relinquishment. Counselling had helped, but in the end it had been the simple command of the Lord to trust him that had brought me to the point of joyful capitulation. At our age, with the decision made, a fair experience of life behind us, and financial security, there seemed to be no point in delaying the event. And so, on a blazingly hot day at the beginning of summer, I became Peter's wife.

Sarah had been delighted with the news. Ruth, true to form, had seemed quietly accepting of the situation, passing little comment, though she had become quite attached to Peter during our courtship, evincing a promising relationship between the two. Although Vicky was enthusiastic in stating her desire to travel down from London for the ceremony, in fact she barely made it in time to the church.

'I can't understand why she couldn't come down and stay with us for a while—get to know Peter and see something of her family,' my mother said in exasperation as she pinned on her corsage. 'She really is the oddest girl.'

Secretly nursing similar thoughts and hurts, I outwardly defended her.

'I believe she said she has a job now. Perhaps she couldn't get time off.'

'Well that's something,' my father remarked. 'What's she doing?'

'Oh . . . only working in a restaurant,' I replied, looking in the mirror as I adjusted the flowers on my hat. 'Waitressing, I think.'

'Sorry I'm late, Mum,' Vicky said breezily as the family prepared to make their way to the church, leaving my father and me to follow. 'I stayed with friends last night and of course missed the bus over this morning. Heavy night, last night.' Her face expressed mock sorrow, as she pirouetted before me. 'Like my dress? It's quite something isn't it? I wanted to look different.'

She looked different, all right. An absolute sight. The garish fabric gathered in flounces and frills, tassles and swathes was more suited to a strip artiste in a seamy show, but she was my daughter and it would have hurt more had she stayed away. Swallowing my distaste and the feelings of grievance, I nodded approval. 'Very nice. But you'll have to hurry or you won't get a lift. You can't very well arrive with me!'

My parents had laid on a superb reception, though we were only family and a few friends on Peter's side. It was their way of setting the seal of approval on our marriage, and I loved them for it. But it was hardly conducive for intimate conversation with one's estranged daughter, and as we left for our honeymoon, I was aware of a great gulf between Vicky and me.

She looked older than her years, the make-up on her face tawdry and cheap. Those few words that had passed between us had been superficialities, and though I had noted Vicky's slurred speech and sleepy eyes, in my naïvety I put it down to drink. Before Peter and I were out of my parents' drive she was donning her coat, evidently intent on leaving the bosom of her family with all haste.

A second Christmas passed in Vicky's absence—the first for Peter and me together. She made every excuse under the sun to explain her inability to come home, settling finally for the one thing over which I had no control.

'Thanks for offering to send the fare, Mum,' she said on the phone 'It's not that. I've got to work. The restaurant's open so someone has to be here.'

Her voice seemed to have softened in recent times, and her manner to be more approachable. There was even a certain charm, a winsomeness in her phraseology, so that her remorse seemed somehow more sincere. 'Perhaps she's geting over her rebellion,' I thought. 'Perhaps, now I'm happily married, we'll all be restored as a united family.'

Certainly, it seemed that Vicky shared my desire. 'I missed you all so much over Christmas,' she wrote early in the New Year. 'I wish I could have come down.'

Grateful for the fact that she had a job at all when so many were unemployed, I could hardly expect her to do other than stick at it.

'I admire her in many ways,' I said to my mother. 'It may not be much of a job, but at least she's not just sitting back and claiming Supplementary Benefit any more. And it must give her some purpose in life. I can think of nothing worse than waking up every morning with nothing to fill the day.'

For weeks, other than the odd three-minute telephone call, there was little in the way of communication. Always rushed, always late in the evening or at expensive times of the day, Vicky's voice on the other end of the line held a note of excitement bordering on the hysterical as she recounted various dubious stories of her life. With no reply to my letters, I had little real knowledge of how she was faring.

Peter had been commuting since our marriage, pending the sale of our respective homes. Shortly before Easter we moved so as to be nearer his work. Ruth was due to go abroad on an exhange during the holidays, necessitating a trip to Heathrow.

'How would you feel,' I asked Peter one morning at breakfast, 'if I combined it with visits to the girls?'

Sarah was still working in London, thought in recent months she had been showing signs of homesickness. While I felt some diffidence in leaving my new husband to fend for himself, it seemed sensible to use the enforced journey to full advantage.

'I think it would be ideal,' he replied in his usual kindly and thoughtful way as he poured milk over his cereal. 'They need to have time alone with you. You know I don't want them to feel I'm always in the way. You go.'

Both girls were absolutely thrilled when I telephoned them that evening, to have the opportunity to show off their respective homes to Ruth and me. Neither had any contact with the other in the city, though with the distances involved and the utter incompatability of their lifestyles, it was hardly surprising. Vicky, if anything, was even more delighted than Sarah, whose flat I had already seen once.

'No one in my family has ever been to stay with me,' Vicky enthused excitedly. Remembering the last time I had visited her locally, I knew a moment's misgiving, but there was so much pathos in her excitement that the momentary revulsion on my part was bathed in guilt. 'I'm going to tell all my friends you're coming,' she continued. 'I can't wait for you to meet Patti, the girl I share with.'

The guilt was magnified. If it meant so much to her why had I not stayed with her before? What a selfish, self-centred mother I must be. Had I been over-preoccupied with my own concerns? Had my needs for Peter's love and companionship blinded me to the needs of my children?

Navigation was not my strong point at the best of times, and this trip was no exception. Despite having lived in and around London throughout my childhood, and made numerous business visits with Jim, it was late by the time Ruth and I found ourselves drawing up outside the blackened and neglected building which bore the address Vicky had given me.

'Well, here we are,' I exclaimed, peering upwards in some distaste.

The whole street had an air of dejectedness, a pitiable apology of habitation for human beings. Drab greyness assaulted eyes used to the vivid greens, blues and golds of open countryside and seaside resort. Even the litter scurried along the gutter as if it wished itself elsewhere. Tired, and somewhat depressed with the prospect of spending the next forty-eight hours in this environment, I got out of the car, clutching my coat around me against the chill of an unseasonable wind.

A huge, old-fashioned door stood open, shedding the last vestiges of paint in profusion to the wind. Joining the dust and dirt on the floor, it rolled in circles in the eddying air, catching occasionally in the grooves and scars of patchy linoleum. A large table littered with uncollected mail was the sole item of furniture; a monument, perhaps, to the apathy of those whose dreary lives were lived out behind the four doors leading off the hall?

'There's a bell here for Flat 3,' Ruth said, rousing me from my speculation. 'Shall I push it?'

'Yes please, darling.' I raised my head in anticipation
of Vicky's appearance on the stairway, and in a moment
or two was rewarded by the sight of her hurrying
downwards, clad in dingy black ski-pants and top, a pair
of down-trodden loafers on her feet.

'I'd just about given you up,' she cried, her voice expressing delight to see us, but tinged with just a hint of
remonstrance. 'You're so late. What happened? Patti
was planning supper an hour ago, and I'm famished.'

'Will the car be all right outside?' I asked, giving her a
hug.

'Oh yes. It's OK till eight in the morning. I'll show you
where to put it later.'

I hastened to point out to Vicky that parking restric-
tions were not my main concern. One heard so many
stories of cars being stripped of wheels, number plates
and mirrors, if not theft of the vehicle itself, but laughing at my fears, Vicky proceeded to lead us up the wide
Victorian staircase.

'I think I'll just bring our luggage in,' I said, turning
back. 'It wouldn't do for Ruth to lose all her stuff before
going abroad.'

'Oh Mum!' Vicky frowned. 'Don't fuss.'

Ruth, who had said nothing, was already at the car,
having taken the keys from my hand, and between us we
unloaded, heaving her heavy suitcase up the stairs.
Vicky paused before a small modern flush door and
rang the bell. Two short, one long.

'Just to let Patti know it's me,' she explained, beaming
at us both. 'We've got a kitten, so we daren't leave the
door open.' She rang the same code again.

The first and second floors bore little evidence of the
former grandeur of street level, and my recent study of
architecture awoke an innate curiosity.

'The landlord packs them in,' Vicky disclosed, seeing
my interest. 'Because the ceilings are so high, he's actually put an extra floor in the building so he could get
more flats in. 'Course, you can't see it from the landings.
That way he gets away with less rates and more rent

without the law knowing anything about it.'

I shook my head in amazement, and evidently pleased with the effect she had achieved in initiating me to the vagaries of a lifestyle so alien to my experience, Vicky launched forth again.

'See this?' She pointed to an apparently recently executed patch on the door. 'That was the police. Raided the joint. Did I tell you about it?'

Her narrative was interrupted at this point by the arrival of Patti at the said door. 'Who's there?' she asked before opening it to admit us.

'You can't be too careful.' She smiled kittenishly, bowing her head so that despite her comparative height she gave the effect of looking up coyly to my five foot two. Warmly she extended a hand to shake my own, welcoming me in and taking a suitcase.

'Did Vicky make you carry this up all on your own?' she asked in little girlish tones. 'Naughty Vicky.'

Wiggling a trim little bottom, clearly outlined by a pair of jeans which must surely have been shrunk on, and which I doubted she could ever be prised out of again, she teetered on four-inch heels down the inner hall.

'Here's your room,' Patti flung open a small twin-bedded room, turning that sweet smile on us once more. 'Me and Vicky sleep here normally, but seeing as you're family we thought we'd give it up for you.'

'Oh, you really shouldn't have gone to all that trouble,' I exclaimed in some embarrassment. 'What will you do?'

'Oh, Vicky and me'll be all right, won't we Vicks?' Reaching out, she put an arm around my daughter's shoulder, pulling her close in an attitude of affection. Flicking back one long curling tress of shining peroxide-blonde hair, she surveyed me from beneath a dark fringe of eyelashes, framing eyes of the most incredible blue. 'I'll leave you now,' she purred. 'Just make your-selves at home while I finish supper.'

'I bet she's a real head-turner with the men,' I thought, as she wiggled out of sight down the hall.

'She's nice, isn't she? Don't you think my flatmate's

nice, Mum?' Vicky spoke for the first time, turning her own green eyes appealingly towards me.

'She seems very nice,' I agreed. In fact I was quite surprised, having seen Vicky's associates of the past. Patti might be a sexpot, but at least she was clean, well mannered and charming. In comparison to Vicky's own grubby appearance and frequent churlishness, Patti could not be thought of as otherwise than a desirable companion for my daughter.

'I was telling you about the police,' Vicky continued, plonking herself on the bed. 'Oh, don't you just love these new duvet covers? I got them last week down the market. I did mean to change the beds for you,' she wrinkled her forehead in consternation, 'but I forgot, I'm afraid. Never mind. They were new last week.'

In dismay, I struggled not to let the feelings of disgust show on my face. A week of Vicky's unwashed body on those sheets was not the most appealing prospect, and I had a strong suspicion that Patti was not above the odd romp with a boyfriend between the covers. Swallowing hard, I took out my comb and began to tidy up my hair.

'Anyway, I was saying,' Vicky resumed, as Ruth began to unzip her case. 'Patti and me got the fright of our lives last week. Seems the police suspected a drugs racket somewhere in the building. They got in through the back door downstairs and were creeping around. We thought someone had broken in and was going to attack us, so we rang the police station. Then they suddenly started hacking down our front door with an axe. Stupid pigs.'

'I suppose they must have had some reason for their suspicions,' I demurred.

'Well they shouldn't terrorize two young, innocent girls, should they?' Vicky shrieked contemptuously, catapulting herself from the bed and making her way out of the door. 'I better help Patti,' she said over one shoulder.

'I shouldn't take anything out of your case, Ruth,' I whispered as she departed. 'And I think we had both better keep our dressing gowns on tonight in bed.' I offered no explanation, but Ruth, obviously sharing my squeamishness, accepted my proposition without argument.

It wasn't that the flat was filthy. It was a far cry from Vicky's previous abode. There had obviously been some attempt made to vaccuum at least those parts of the carpet which showed. But surveying the range of cosmetics which all but obliterated the dusty surface of the big old mahogany dressing-table, and the miniscule items of underwear which festooned its Victorian embellishments, I was becoming increasingly convinced as to Patti's state of unchastity. It is quite commonplace these days for girls to have several sexual relationships going at once. That was her business, and none of my affair. But the thought that Ruth and I were going to have to sleep the next two nights in her bed didn't make me feel easy.

Deliberately putting the thought from my mind, Ruth and I left the bedroom and went in search of the kitchen from which came an appetizing aroma. Patti was actually in the process of serving up pork chops, mashed potato, mushrooms and peas as we entered.

'That looks good,' I said encouragingly. 'It'll be nice to eat something I haven't had to shop for and cook myself.'

'I thought you probably hadn't had much for lunch,' Patti smiled, 'so pork chops seemed a good idea.'

'Lovely,' I agreed. 'Do you take it in turns to do the cooking?'

'No . . .' Patti licked her fingers, her tongue darting in and out just like that of the kitten which was exploring the left-overs in the pot-filled sink. 'Vicky wouldn't eat at all if I didn't cook for her. She really needs someone to look after her,' A conspiratorial tone came into her voice. 'I do my best to take care of her—but you know what she's like.'

It was funny, I mused, how people always wanted to take care of Vicky. Melanie had seen herself in collusion with me in the task of seeing to Vicky's welfare; so too had the skinhead at the court. A mixture of admiration and exasperation filled me. Why ever couldn't Vicky take care of herself? It seemed an affront to her dignity. Or was this more a matter of manipulation: convincing others of her inadequacy and thus indulging a lazy streak?

The meal was eaten in the sitting-room, balanced on our knees as we watched a quiz show on television. Vicky picked at her food, her feelings of being famished evidently now quenched. With still half the contents of her plate untouched, she lit up a cigarette, using an expensive gold lighter. I wondered how she managed on a waitress's wage. The ash-trays were overflowing. Both girls smoked heavily, and the acrid smell of stale nicotine pervaded the atmosphere.

'It's a good clear picture,' I said, in reference to the television. 'Good colour too.'

'Yeah,' Vicky replied absent-mindedly, tucking her grubby bare feet beneath her on the settee. 'A bloke at work gave it to me.'

'Gosh,' I exclaimed, 'you must give good service to get tips like that.'

She smiled, turning in my direction, but it was as if she'd almost forgotten Ruth's and my presence and was vaguely surprised to see us there. 'The hi-fi's Patti's,' she said, apropos of nothing.

'You must have a good job,' I said conversationally, addressing myself to Patti. 'What do you do?'

Patti pressed her full red lips together, bowing her head and smiling coyly from doe eyes. 'I haven't actually got a job at the moment, Mrs Scott,' she said apologetically, holding her plate out for the kitten to lick.

I lay awake a long time that night, pondering the logic of two girls in the East End, in menial employment or none at all, who could afford such luxury consumables, while Sarah in the West End, in a position of responsibility and prestige, barely managed to make ends meet. Wrapping my feet in my nightie, and straightening the

towel I had put over the pillow, I fell at last into an
uneasy sleep.

I was awakened in the morning by the ringing of the
telephone. It had been going non-stop all the previous
evening, and again I wondered how they managed to
pay the bills.

'It was cut off not long ago,' Vicky told me in high
dudgeon over breakfast. 'It wasn't our fault. That stupid
landlord, with his great fat pig of a wife, put our rent up
without even telling us. 'Course that meant the phone
money had to go to him instead of paying the bill. It was
nearly two hundred pounds last quarter. A girl Patti
knows ran it all up ringing her boyfriend in Morocco.
She wouldn't pay either. Cow!'

She rambled on for a while, before lapsing eventually
into a morose silence. 'She hasn't changed,' I thought.
'It's still Vicky versus the world.'

'You look tired,' I remarked, clearing the dishes to
join those from last night.

'Didn't sleep well,' she mumbled, struggling to keep
her eyes open. 'Here, let me.' She made a feeble attempt
to push me to one side as I ran hot water into the sink.
'Said I'd do it last night, but I forgot.'

'Are you feeling all right?' I asked anxiously, putting
one hand on her forehead. 'You're not sickening for
anything are you?'

'I'm all right, Mum.' Angrily she pushed my hand
away.

'Why don't you get ready so we can do all the trips we
planned today, while I finish here?' I said firmly.

After my bath, taken in the same gingerly fashion as
my night's sleep in someone else's bed, Ruth and I made
our way to the lounge to await Vicky.

'Oh, I'm sorry,' I apologized as we entered the room.
'I didn't realize you had guests.'

Patti, still clad in nothing more than her baby-doll
pyjamas, was seated cross-legged on the floor. The
ravages of yesterday's make-up and her unruly hair
tumbling down her back seemed not to bother her one

whit. The inevitable cigarette in one hand, she was busily engaged in counting out a huge pile of five- and ten-pound notes, while around her, occupying all the chairs, three or four leather-clad youths added their contribution to the density of the atmosphere. Of Vicky there was no sign.

'I only make it four hundred and fifty, Vince.' Pausing only long enough to acknowledge our presence, Patti continued with the business at hand. Was it my imagination, or had a hard, almost threatening note crept into her mellifluous voice?

Rousing himself from the general air of apathy which seemed to have taken hold of the youths, one detached himself from the others and ground out a cigarette in the ash-tray.

'I swear it was five hundred, Patti,' he said with as much vehemence as he could muster.

Vicky appeared at the door, 'Ready?' she enquired.

'What was all that about?' I asked casually as we walked briskly down the stairs and out into the cold spring morning.

'Patti's just sold her old hi-fi,' she said in an off-hand manner as she headed towards the underground. 'She's saving for a car.'

'She does very well for someone out of work,' I said tartly, raising one eyebrow.

'She's got a wealthy Arab boyfriend,' Vicky replied.

Something just didn't ring true. Somehow I couldn't quite put my finger on it. Deep in thought, I followed the girls as we set off for Madame Tussaud's.

PART 2

Darkness Revealed

10

Binding and Loosing

Looking back to that visit as I received the fateful tele-phone call from Vicky the following Christmas, many of the inconsistencies gradually began to fall into place, though it was to be some time before all was revealed. We'd heard little of her since Ruth and I had stayed—hence my surprise at her midnight call. The shock was numbing as she broke the news of her heroin addiction. We had just settled it that I would ask my parents if she could stay with them over Christmas.

'But don't tell Aunty Pat and Sally, or the rest of the family,' she pleaded. 'And Mum . . . could you ring Dr Engles to see if he'll help? You can get methadone to get you off smack.'

The jargon was lost on me. I had a lot to learn. True to my word, I planned, as I saw Peter and Ruth off next morning, to telephone my parents and the doctor. My first call, however, in an attempt to answer the questions raised during my sleepless night, was one of our church elders.

'Oh Gerald, I've had a dreadful night,' I explained, my voice weary with fatigue as I filled in the details. 'It just keeps going round and round in my mind that in not wanting my second pregnancy so soon after the first, I actually rejected Vicky in the womb. Gerald, I just

wonder if this is the culmination of that rejection. And if
Satan has had an exceptional influence in her life because of it, then could Vicky's drug problem be our
fault?

Close to tears as I contemplated this thought and
grappled with its implications, I continued my reasoning. 'After all, most believing parents dedicate their children in some way to the Lord, trusting that he will
protect and guide them, leading them into all truth.
Since neither Jim nor I wanted Vicky, we must surely
have abandoned her to the Enemy.'

I'd tossed and turned all night wrestling with the
problem. Now I hoped for some answers.

'Scripture says that what we bind on earth shall be
bound in heaven, and what we loose on earth shall be
loosed in heaven,' (Matthew 16:19 and 18:18) Gerald's
kindly voice replied. 'If there is any possibility of Vicky
having been oppressed from the time of her conception,
we can use the authority vested in us by Jesus to cut her
loose.'

Hadn't I done that when I'd worked back through the
past? My befuddled mind struggled to break through to
lucidity.

'I did pray that all three girls would be healed from
any and all harm done to them in the past, either by me
or their father,' I said desperately.

'And so they will be.' His voice carried a note of encouragement and authority, brooking no room for
doubt. 'But now we're going to cut Vicky off so that she
will be free to choose. We can't make her choose the
Lord's way; she has free will like we all do. But if her
free will has been taken over by the Enemy in the past,
we can restore her to a position of free choice once
more.' He paused. 'Do you understand that, Meggie?'

'Oh yes,' I replied.

This was not a new concept to me. We had, since our
move nine months previously, been attending the large
baptist church which had been Peter's spiritual home for
the past twenty years. But I had received ample teaching

in my last fellowship concerning the matters of which Gerald spoke, and it made good sense to me. To believe that our minds may be influenced only for good by the indwelling of the Holy Spirit, and that failing that we are free spirits on whom no doctrine is writ, can be nothing short of a travesty of the truth. We ignore the devil at our peril.

Huge chunks of Jesus' teaching and the apostolic doctrine—all the inspiration of God— are given to put us on our guard that what is not voluntarily submitted to the Lord, may be claimed by the Enemy.

'Father,' Gerald prayed, as I sat on the stairs clutching the telephone, 'in the strong name of Jesus, and in the power vested in us by that name, we cut Vicky off from any influence of the Enemy, and we loose her on earth and in heaven to have freedom of choice. Father, we cannot determine that choice, but we ask that her mind be clear and liberated from the dulling effect of drugs, and that by your Spirit you will lead her into all truth.'

Though my heart was still heavy in anticipation of all that lay before me, it was with considerable relief that I thanked Gerald and bade him goodbye. It was tempting to ask, 'Why God? Why me? Why my daughter?' But the vision of Vicky at the water's edge had shown her being lifted in a net while all the dross fell away. This, I was sure, was an unavoidable part of that process. There could be no escaping it if she were ever to stand in the hand of the Lord.

The next call had to be to my parents. Despite Vicky's initial demand that I tell no one of her condition, I'd insisted that they had the right to decide for themselves whether or not she should be allowed to come into their home. There was little doubt in my mind as to how they would feel, and I was thus saved the agony of what I should do if they refused. Nevertheless, it was with some trepidation that I dialled the number.

'Oh Meggie. . . .' The prolonged exhalation and momentary loss of words told me all I needed to know of my mother's emotions as I gave the news as briefly and gently as was possible. In my mind's eye I could see the strain etched in the contours of her face, concern dulling her alert grey eyes. A moment of anger, its brevity as fleeting as its intensity, shot through me. Why did Vicky have to inflict so much pain and anguish on those who loved her? In the next moment I knew that love, by its very definition, carries pain as a part of its fabric, the warp and the weft each dependent on the other for its very structure.

'I shall understand if you don't want her to come,' I said, my voice sounding strangely flat and unemotional, though in reality the struggle not to break down was almost more than I could bear. 'I wouldn't hold it against you in any way,' I continued assuringly. 'It must be your decision. Vicky knows that.'

'How could we turn her away?' my mother asked. 'I'll speak to your father, but I'm sure he'll agree. She's our own flesh and blood.'

In moments she'd rung back with the answer. There'd been no question on my father's part either. Vicky was to come home, to be loved, to be accepted, to be helped in any way possible.

'We shan't say anything to the others,' my parents assured me. 'Nor shall we say anything to Vicky unless she opens up the opportunity. We'll abide by whatever you think best.'

Non-Christians they might be, but the Lord had undoubtedly blessed me greatly in his choice of parents for me. Gulping down the lump in my throat, I thanked him for his love shown to me in this way. Would that Vicky had known such a home as mine.

Dr Engles was an old friend. His shock and sympathy when I rang the health centre after the call to my parents was as real as Gerald's had been, but his counsel, delivered in the light of his medical experience, and with no Christian principles brought to bear, was utterly different.

'I'm so sorry, Meg,' he replied when I got through to the surgery. 'It's a devastating situation to be in. I know you want to help Vicky all you can, but I have to tell you that most heroin addicts are beyond help.'

My heart beat fast, a leaden weight somewhere in the pit of my stomach. I shook my head, a wry smile playing on my lips. He meant well, but he couldn't possibly understand. It would be unfair to expect him to. As a non-Christian, how could he have any comprehension of the reality of a promise of God, given in the form of a vision of Vicky paddling on the water's edge and being lifted into the palm of God's hand?

'She's coming home for Christmas,' I demurred, 'She wants help to come off the heroin.'

'Meg.' The distrust was evident in the single word. 'They all say they want to come off, but when it actually comes down to it, very few really do. They just cause a lot of misery and heartache to their families in the meantime.'

'My parents are quite happy for her to stay over Christmas so that she can be with the family.' I was getting a bit fed up with his attitude. Other addicts may not succeed in coming off, but they didn't have the benefit of a loving family and the supreme weapon of prayer.

'And what about Peter?' Dr Engles asked. 'How does he feel about it? I don't want to be hard or make life more difficult for you Meg, but you've only been married . . . what, eighteen months or so? I've heard of marriages being broken up and whole families falling apart because of trying to help a heroin addict. You surely don't want to put your relationship under that sort of strain?'

Peter and I had talked until late into the night after Vicky's bombshell had been delivered. If my first thought had been to help her, my second thought had been to query his reactions. Vicky was not his flesh and blood, and though he'd known of her trouble with the police, he could hardly have bargained for this sort of responsibility when marrying me.

'We married for better or worse,' he'd said, holding me tight as we'd sat up in bed. 'This must be part of the worse. Bit earlier than we might have expected, but there you are.' He shrugged a shoulder, looking down at me, a smile touching his lips. 'We have been praying for Vicky haven't we? Perhaps this is an answer to those prayers that she would turn back to her family after the estrangement of the past few years.'

Perhaps Peter was right. Jesus always met people at their point of need. Perhaps Vicky had had to sink this low to recognize her need, and perhaps, having recognized it, she would now allow Jesus to reach out and touch her, to restore and renew her.

'She mentioned metha-something as a means of getting off the heroin,' I continued to Dr Engles. 'Can you prescribe that for her?'

'I can't promise anything, Meg, but I'll certainly see her,' he replied. 'Ring the surgery for an appointment when she's home next week.'

The day passed in a fuzz of unreality, anchored only by slender threads of prayer to the supremacy of a God who works all things together for good (Romans 8:28). As last evening came, and I was able to speak to Vicky once more when she rang from work.

'We all want you home for Christmas,' I told her in response to her eager but fearful plea to know the verdict. 'But Vicky—no . . . no needles.' I swallowed hard, almost choking over the word and trying unsuccessfully to block out of my mind visions of my daughter piercing her skin to inject poison into her veins. 'It would be too dangerous with the little ones around,' I concluded, in reference to my young nieces.

'Oh don't worry, Mum,' the relief was evident in Vicky's breathless response. 'I won't inject, I promise. But Mum,' she paused, 'I've got an appointment to see a doctor up here in the New Year. He'll give me methadone to get me off the heroin. But till then I'll have to have something. Did you speak to Dr Engles?'

'Yes. He says he'll see you but he doesn't promise to give you anything.' No point in telling her everything else he'd said.

'I'll have to snort then,' she said a trifle hysterically, 'but I promise I won't take much.'

There it was again. A whole new language. I'd have to ask her the meaning of all these terms, but not now, not while she was on such a knife-edge of resolution. She could still fall either way, and I was aware of the tight-rope I must walk in order not to push her off in the wrong direction.

'I wonder what the legal implications are?' my father pondered when I told him of the conversation with Vicky. 'We would probably be guilty of aiding and abetting in having Vicky here knowing she's taking drugs.'

'I must confess, I feel very ignorant,' I admitted. 'It's like a whole new world to me. I don't even understand half the terminology, let alone the legal, moral, medical or any other implications.'

'Well one thing we know,' he said cynically, 'she hasn't obtained her heroin legally, and that only leaves criminal means.'

'You mean on the black market?' I asked naïvely.

'That, or other ways,' he replied darkly, refusing to be drawn any further.

'He must mean stealing,' I thought, 'like she did from the back of the lorry, and breaking and entering the health centre.'

It was hardly the happiest of Christmases. Probably less so, in fact, than those when Vicky had been absent. We were all trying so hard—trying to treat Vicky normally so as not to upset her or cause my sisters any suspicions, yet trying, at the same time, to show her how much we all cared, loved her, accepted her and wanted to help her back to health and wholeness. So much trying was . . . trying, to say the least! And futile too. The strains and tensions of those of us in the know, inevitably communicated themselves to the uninitiated. There was the tangible evidence, too, of a forgotten square of foil left in the bathroom, the pungent smell of a burnt-out match mingling with the sweet lingering scent of. . .? You wouldn't know, unless you knew. But it didn't take long to guess, and to guess with the accuracy born of a mental analysis of all one had read and heard or seen in picture form in newspaper and on television.

Shock began to register on the faces of my sisters and their husbands as the gradual realization of what was unfurling before their eyes began to grip the mind. Pat, my middle sister, was the first.

'Vicky's on drugs, isn't she?' she asked in hushed and horrified tones.

'Yes.' It could not be denied. It wouldn't be fair. The speculation had to be ended. 'She didn't want anyone to know. She's coming home to us after Christmas to come off.'

'Well it's obvious isn't it?' Pat sat in the chair opposite me in my parents' lounge, her feet tucked up beneath her, a worried frown between her eyes. 'She looks dreadful. Ill. Really ill.'

'Yes.' I nodded my head. There was little to add.

'How long has she been on it?' Pat asked.

'Two years.' I twisted my hands together in my lap. 'Dr Engles says that's about as long as you can live, mainlining.'

'What does that mean? Injecting?' Pat leaned forwards in her chair, intent on my answer.

'Straight into the veins, I understand.' A shiver ran through my body.

'Poor thing.' Tears began to fill Pat's quiet grey eyes. 'I think she's always been jealous of the other two. It's hard being the middle one.'

'Could you talk to her do you think?' I leaned forwards, regarding my sister intently. 'Let her know you understand. Get alongside her so she doesn't feel so isolated; so she feels she has a real friend and confidante.'

'Yes,' Pat nodded, blinking hard. 'I've always felt sorry for her. The eldest seems to occupy a special place, and the youngest's just the baby. The middle one doesn't seem to fit in anywhere.'

As the festival progressed, even the children began to notice.

'Why does Vicky keep disappearing, Mummy?' my eldest niece asked her mother, looking askance at Vicky whose bent little body shuffled across the room, her eyes dull and glazed beneath the drooping lids, a seemingly beatific smile on her face.

'She just likes to have a cigarette,' Pat explained briskly, 'and since none of us smokes, she goes elsewhere so as not to bother us.'

'She goes to the bathroom,' the youngest niece whispered. 'I know, I looked through the keyhole.'

This piece of fantasy passed unnoticed. There were no keyholes in my parents' home. But Vicky's condition continued to be very much in the forefront of attention, with everyone putting on a false air of jollity to conceal the real atmosphere of despondency and despair.

'It's nice to have you back with us after the last few Christmases away,' my father said, giving her a bear hug and stroking down the wild, unbrushed hair.

Vicky pushed him away, and I saw the hurt register in his eyes.

'He's only trying to let you know how much he cares,' I protested.

'You know I can't bear being touched, Mum.' Vicky's eyes filled with tears, while her voice held that same note of near-hysteria. 'I can't help it.'

'Come on, Vicky,' my mother said in the no-nonsense voice she'd used on my sisters and me as children. 'Go and get your hair brushed, there's a good girl.'

Surprisingly, Vicky complied, though there was little evidence in the end result. But while she seemed to respond to my mother's assumed bossiness, her relationship with me became increasingly tense. Was it my difficulty in coping with the dichotomy of loyalties between my parents and my child? Or was it jealousy on her part, of the easy relationships enjoyed between myself and her sisters?

'Her room is disgusting,' my mother complained, her nose wrinkling up as the acrid odour of stale nicotine wafted from numerous overflowing ash-trays and dirty cups and saucers. 'I do think she could at least make her bed and empty the ash-trays.'

'I'll do it,' I replied, anxious to burden them no further.

'No,' my father replied. 'She has to learn to clear up her own mess.'

'Oh don't nag, Mum', Vicky responded, her voice sounding unutterably tired as she slurred the words together.

Something had to be done. We couldn't go on like this. I hoped that Dr Engles would be able to offer some sort of help.

I I

'I Don't Want to Die'

Several questions were, in fact, answered when we visited Dr Engles one bright and sunny morning between Christmas and the New Year.

'Will you come in with me please, Mum?' Vicky asked nervously as we approached the health centre for her appointment.

Then I realized that this was where she'd acted as lookout for the gang who'd broken in and stolen drugs. She must be wondering what sort of reception she'd be getting.

In fact, the doctor made not even a slanting reference to the event, greeting us both as the friends we were. But when it came to offering the practical help Vicky demanded, his refusal was polite but firm.

'This doctor you've been seeing . . .' he leaned forwards on his desk, regarding Vicky encouragingly, 'will you tell me his name?'

'I don't think that matters,' she said sullenly.

'Well, Vicky, there are doctors and there are doctors.' He sat back once more, 'Some are pretty unscrupulous you know. Your mother mentioned the name of a doctor you had told her was treating a friend of yours. I took the trouble to make enquiries and it seems he has a court case pending for alleged malpractice.'

'Really?' My mouth dropped open in amazement.

The doctor turned towards me. 'We get a few foreign doctors—some whose qualifications wouldn't stand up in this country—who take a time-share in rooms and set up in practice. You might have a doctor's surgery in the morning, naturopath in the afternoon, and a guru in the evening. They share the costs and the facilities. They're not all quacks, of course, but there is the occasional dubious character.'

My illusions destroyed, Dr Engles turned his attention back to Vicky. 'You'll kill yourself if you go on like this you know, Vicky. Heroin abuse will destroy your kidneys, liver and veins. There's only one way to come off and that's to make up your mind and do it. Taking methadone isn't really the answer. Are you still injecting?'

'No. Snorting and chasing the dragon.' The hostility was building up.

'That's sniffing the powder like snuff, and inhaling the fumes when it's heated on foil,' the doctor said for my benefit, then turning back to Vicky, 'Well that destroys the membranes of your nose, you know.' The doctor frowned. 'Are you taking anything else—amphetamines, alcohol?'

Vicky shrugged. 'Speed, sometimes.'

'So you're mixing them?' Dr Engles raised his eyebrows. 'That can be lethal.'

The longer he questioned her, the more withdrawn Vicky became. Eventually, after taking urine samples, looking in her eyes and taking her blood pressure, the doctor ushered us out with the offer of further counselling should we require it. But still he maintained a definite refusal to prescribe methadone.

Vicky was close to tears as we stepped into the bright sunshine. 'Fat lot of help he was,' she said bitterly.

'Shall we go for a drive?' I suggested, feeling desperately sorry for her. I was sure the doctor was right, but could imagine that to Vicky it must have seemed like a door slamming in her face. Whatever happened, I had to help her. Her life expectancy had been spelled out in no uncertain terms.

We parked the car in an isolated spot overlooking the beach, and for a few moments sat in silence, enjoying the winter solitude and soporific warmth of the sun's rays on the car. Overhead a couple of gulls wheeled and dipped, shrieking raucously.

'Oh Mum, I'm so frightened,' Vicky turned suddenly towards me, tears streaming down her face. The unexpected outburst startled me. 'I don't want to die. I don't want to die. Please help me . . . help me. . . .'

The hard look had gone from her face and beside me sat a terrified child. For some minutes she cried, allowing me only to cover her hand with mine. Then, 'I've been mainlining for two or three years,' she wept. 'I just can't seem to stop. I've tried and tried.'

'Darling, we'll give you all the help and support you need.' Tears sprang to my eyes as I surveyed her crumpled little face.

'The doctor I saw before coming home will give me a prescription privately without me having to register. If I go up to get it, can I come back to stay with you till I'm off?'

'Are you sure that's the answer, Vicky? You heard what Dr Engles said.'

'Mum,' her voice took on the strident note of hysteria. 'Have you ever seen someone come off cold turkey? It's hell! I've got to have methadone.'

I turned away towards the window, momentarily shutting my eyes against the scene of sun, sand and sea. 'Please Lord, help me to help her.'

''Course, in some ways it's just been too easy for me,' Vicky broke into the silence, a further outburst of tears poured from her swollen eyes. 'All my friends spend their whole lives wrapped up in worrying about where the next fix'll come from. They spend all day nicking things—shop-lifting, picking pockets and so on—just so's they can sell it to buy more smack.'

A renewed attack of sobbing racked her body. 'I want you to know, Mum, I've never had to be a prostitute to get my stuff. You do believe me, don't you? I never had to sell my body.'

'Oh, Vicky!' With tears streaming down my face, we collapsed into each other's arms, the first natural and unrestrained embrace we'd shared for years. For some moments the car shook in gentle rhythm as we both sobbed together. Was this what my father had been alluding to when he'd spoken of the ways open to finance an addiction? Did he believe Vicky was prostituting herself to pay for her habit? How naïve I had been not even letting it occur to me!

'That's part of the trouble, really,' Vicky continued, drawing away, immense sadness etched into her face. 'Patti supplied all my junk. I just went home every week and handed over all my wages and she gave me all I needed.' Understanding began to register in my eyes. 'She really looked after me you know, Mum. She really cared for me. But p'raps if I'd not had it so easy, if I'd had to get it the hard way, I wouldn't have got so hooked.'

'Vicky,' I exclaimed, horror and revulsion swelling my voice, 'don't you see? She didn't care for you. Not really. She was only after you for your money. It was in her interest to keep you supplied.'

'No, you're wrong, Mum. You don't understand. Patti's a real friend to me. You saw how she looked after me.'

'How much did you have to give her?' I asked, further realization dawning on me.

'Three or four hundred a week.' Vicky shrugged it off as if it were pence she was speaking of.

'Pounds?' I gasped. 'Where ever. . .?'

'I can earn that easy.' Was there a note of pride in her voice?

'What sort of restaurant is it that you work in?' I asked.

She opened the window, drawing her cigarettes from her bag. 'May I?' she asked, striking a match as I nodded a reply.

'It's a club really,' she explained, drawing deeply on the smoke. 'You get these dirty old men coming in expecting . . . you know. We get them to buy drinks for us—really expensive ones. We don't serve alcohol, but they'll pay pounds for fruit cocktails just to have our company *and* give us good tips.' Vicky flicked ash out of the window, her face lighting up as a new thought occurred to her. 'And Mum, we have the prettiest little uniform—all frilly and short. You should see me in mine. I look really good, even though I say it myself.'

I thought my heart would break with the pathos of the moment. Somehow, her delight in how she looked, the very fact that she wanted to look pretty, coupled with her feelings about men, spoke more clearly to me of her distorted state of mind than anything. 'Oh Lord, what's happened to her that she can't even differentiate between real caring and a cunning, self-seeking and sick counterfeit, nor between real self-esteem and this shameful and disgusting sham?'

'And these men will really buy non-alcoholic drinks costing pounds a glass just for the pleasure of your company?' I asked in disbelief.

'Oh, yeah.' Vicky drew deeply on her cigarette, blowing the smoke from her mouth in disdain as she tossed the stub from the window. 'They're disgusting—like all men.' Her voice took on the hard tone of utter loathing. 'You just lead them on—build them up a bit—then walk off.' Her head came up in an attitude of pride as if what she had just described warranted a pat on the back. 'Serves them right. They always come back—hoping there's more. Sometimes they want photograph sessions upstairs—posing with the girls. That makes a bit more money.'

I'd heard enough and could bear no more.

'Vicky,' I took her hands in mine and looked her straight in the eye. 'No matter what you've done, I love you. Do you understand that?' I waited till she smiled wanly. 'And no matter what you've done, Jesus loves you. He can forgive you and make you clean again, washing all of the past away. You only have to ask him.'

Gently, she removed her hands. 'Oughtn't we to be getting back?' she asked, turning straight ahead and winding up the side window. Sighing deeply, I started the car.

Thinking about it as I lay in bed that night, it all fell into place. The police raid at Vicky's London flat, 'terrorizing two young innocent girls'. The coded ringing of the doorbell. The expensive hi-fi equipment, colour TV, gold lighter—even the new duvet covers. All stolen property, no doubt. And the money changing hands. Patti must be a pusher. I hated her with all the energy I could muster, my heart feeling as if it would burst with so much feeling swelling within it. And then I shot up in bed, my hands clammy, my heart beating wildly. Patti and Vicky had travelled to India together only that summer, with the former's 'wealthy Arab boyfriend'. Was Vicky being drawn in deeper than even she realized?

Not if I had anything to do with it!

It would not be true to say that there had been no doubts as to whether Vicky would return after she had travelled back to London. I had immediately enlisted the prayer support of all my trusted Christian friends, aware of the fact that this was no time for scruples. Just as Moses had needed support as his hands were lifted to the Lord by trusted friends during the battle against the Amalekites (Exodus 17:12) so I too, bowed down with emotional fatigue, needed that same degree of succour.

It was with relief, therefore, that I collected her from the bus depot one afternoon a couple of weeks after the New Year. An air of bright determination and hope lifted the ravaged youthful lines of her face, going some way to filling out the haggard contours. Her eyes still bore the unmistakable fetters of heroin, shackling her to that counterfeit heaven now discovered to be hell.

'I've just had my last fix,' she greeted me cheerfully, her speech slurred and stance unsteady. 'Easy enough to be optimistic,' I thought, 'while still under the influence. It would be the next few hours, days and weeks which would be most telling.'

'D'you know what my prescription cost?' she demanded indignantly as we stowed her meagre belongings in the boot of the car. 'Fifty quid! *Fifty quid!* And I had to pay another eighty for blood tests.'

We fixed her up with a Christian friend who was a chemist, allowing Vicky to pay for the private prescription herself. The money she earned in so disreputable a way might as well be put to good use in procuring for her a more promising way of life.

'What exactly is methadone?' I asked her.

'It's a substitute for heroin,' she explained as she poured the sticky green syrup into a spoon. 'You have to register with the Home Office to get it. Unless you beat the system, like I did, and go privately.'

'Don't you just replace one addiction with another?' I let the duplicity of 'beating the system' pass unmentioned.

'You could. But they give you a reducing dose. 'Course, you can get it on the black market. People sell it and use the money to buy the real thing.'

I was learning, and fast.

As Peter and I sat in bed talking that night, he asked, 'Are you going to suggest any sort of programme for her future?'

'You mean moving away from London and trying for some more qualifications to help her get a job? No, not yet. I think we've got to tackle one thing at a time.'

'Yes, I agree.' Peter nodded sagely. 'Much better to take a step at a time or she'll feel so overwhelmed she'll give up.'

'How have you found her?' I pulled my dressing-gown about my shoulders.

'You may well ask.' He smiled wryly in the lamplight. 'Of course, I hardly know her. I'm going to have to build up a whole relationship with her from scratch. As far as she's concerned I'm a complete stranger, and I can see her looking at me as if trying to weigh up whether I'm to be trusted or not.'

'Mmmm. But surely she'll see how good a relationship you have with Sarah and Ruth?'

'That may not be altogether helpful,' Peter replied, pursing his lips. 'Still, we have made a beginning. The one thing I know we share in common is a love of cats, and since I feed ours—or rather Vicky's before she left home—it's proved a useful topic for bridge-building.'

Praising God once more for his provision in blessing me with a husband like Peter, I settled down, after we'd prayed, in an easier frame of mind.

It was not to last. Throughout the night, and for the succeeding weeks, Vicky prowled the house, raiding the freezer, the biscuit tin and the bread bin, making coffee and smoking incessantly. Unable to sleep, I would join her downstairs on numerous occasions, silently praying that this spirit of restlessness be bound and she be filled with peace. Keeping my conversation light, I sought to distract her, but without success. Increasingly, fatigue robbed me of my own ability to cope.

'What worries me is that we'll all be burned in our beds,' Peter sighed as we lay awake night after night. 'I don't want to come on 'heavy' with her—she hardly knows me—but I do think you should tell her not to smoke in bed.'

And so I did, but to no avail. A night or two later, roused from my sleep for no apparent reason, I found myself walking towards Vicky's room. It didn't take long to know why. Mouth open, her bedding tangled up with arms and legs, Vicky lay fast asleep. In her hand, resting on the bottom sheet, was a burning cigarette.

'Praise God,' I told Peter. 'The Lord must have got me up. There was no other reason for me to have woken.'

Only a dull brown mark on the sheet convinced Vicky next morning, as I admonished her and put an absolute veto on all smoking in the house. 'It could just as easily happen in an easy chair in the lounge,' I said, 'You'll have to go into the conservatory or garden in future for a cigarette.'

Every night after that we prayed, in the authority of

Jesus' name, that the Enemy might be bound and that we might know the continuing protection of the Lord.

'I'm going to have to see the doctor,' Vicky told me one morning. 'I didn't tell you before, because I didn't want to worry you, but I had to go into hospital just before coming home. I've got an ulcer on my leg and it needs draining and packing.'

'An ulcer?' my mother cried when I conveyed this news to her over the telephone. 'Oh, Meggie. My mother had leg ulcers, but she was an old woman and diabetic at that. How appalling that Vicky should have them at her age.'

After the first visit to our GP—a new one, since we had moved only the previous year—Vicky was referred to the nurse. A new awareness had come upon me since the court case when the skinhead had approached me, as to how others saw a drug addict, and the looks of mingled pity and disgust given by those who saw her sorry state did not pass unnoticed. Was this how lepers had been viewed in Jesus' day?

'Would you like me to come with you?' I asked her. It seemed to me that in accompanying her I would be endorsing her personhood, establishing her in the eyes of those who saw her as a young woman with a mother and family who loved her and cared for her, rather than as an object of revulsion and abhorrence—a statistic in that hazy, otherworldness of drug abuse.

Those feelings were present in the eyes of the nurse, together with condemnation—and I couldn't blame her —as she surveyed the smelly and suppurating ulcer which had eaten into Vicky's flesh. 'Is this from the needle?' she asked, her nose and lip wrinkling in distaste.

Vicky nodded. 'I can't use my arms any more,' she said.

'Well, the doctor's told me to take blood and urine samples,' the older woman stated as she drained and cleaned the open wound, using forceps and rubber gloves to wipe the antiseptic-soaked cotton-wool over the area. Deftly packing it with a gauze strip, and leaving a 'wick' to continue the draining action, she showed Vicky how to perform the task upon herself.

'This is going to have to be done every day. Do you think you can manage on your own till the end of the week?'

Assuring her that she could, Vicky was despatched to produce the urine sample, leaving me the opportunity to talk alone with the nurse and thus establish a bond of mutual caring which I hoped would be beneficial to Vicky.

I was shocked at the sight of my daughter's bruised and blackened legs which were usually clad in brightly coloured tights, but found that reaction a mild foretaste of the feeling engendered in me at the sight of her arms. She'd kept them carefully concealed until this time, but as I watched the nurse trying valiantly to take blood from veins whose walls were so obviously broken down, it was only by a supreme act of will that I did not break down myself. Was this the young flesh that God had knit together in my womb; the frame he created in the secret place when his eyes perceived that unformed body so fearfully and wonderfully made? (Psalm 139: 13–16).

Later that night I recounted the episode to Peter. 'Only last week,' I added, 'I met Mrs Soames at the bus stop. You remember her. She's ninety-seven and still buses into town every week to have lunch with a friend.'

'Doesn't she live at the old people's home down the road?' Peter asked, breaking into a smile as he recalled. 'Nice old girl. As lively as a cricket, isn't she?'

'That's the one,' I nodded. 'Well, she was telling me that the surgeon advised her to have her toes off so she could wear prettier shoes. They're very arthritic,' I explained as Peter gave me a puzzled frown. '"What would I want with prettier shoes?" she asked me. "I'd rather have my toes." There she is, hanging on to useless, painful old toes when Vicky is abusing and destroying the youthful flesh of only twenty years or so.'

The more I thought and prayed about it, the more I

realized that you cannot judge a drug addict by normal standards. I'd heard it argued that the comparison between the lepers of Jesus' era and the drug addicts of today is ill-founded, since the former were the innocent victims of disease whereas the drug abuser is the victim only of his own actions. In other words, he chooses to be a drug addict. But is it as simple as that?

We all have freedom of choice, but the Bible is quite catagorical in stating that in *not* choosing righteousness through Jesus, the choice is automatically made for the other side. 'He who is not with me is against me' (Matthew 12:30) Jesus said, thus demonstrating that there is no 'no-man's-land'. 'You are slaves,' the Bible says 'to the one whom you obey,' and prior to deciding for the Lord, we are all 'slaves to sin' (Romans 6:16,17).

A slave has no say in the running of his life. In the battle for spiritual supremacy, Satan seeks to control the lives of God's creatures, making them over into his own evil image instead of that of the Creator. As Paul reminds us: 'Our struggle is not against flesh and blood, but against the . . . powers of this dark world and against the spiritual forces of evil in the heavenly realms' (Ephesians 6:12).

The sad thing is, that unless a deliberate act of surrender is made to Christ (or, in the case of Satanism, to the devil), the unbeliever is quite unaware of his automatic conscription to the Enemy's batallions, since he has no spiritual perception. The comparative lack of any sort of spiritual awareness so prevalent in the twentieth century makes the youngster of today vulnerable in the extreme. His mind may be taken over by the Enemy without his even being aware of the fact. Drugs must surely, in this day and age, be one of Satan's most successful weapons in controlling the minds and lives of those who believe themselves to have freedom of choice.

Armed though I was with this spiritual insight, when an opportunity presented itself later in the week for a ministry of deliverance, I felt that this was not necessarily the best thing for Vicky. An itinerant Christian healer was visiting the vicinity, but my initial inclination to take Vicky was shrouded in doubt, particularly when I heard words of caution from all those church leaders whom I most trusted.

'Surely if this person were to minister deliverance to Vicky, there's the possibility that she might end up worse off than before?' I asked one of our elders. 'I mean, Scripture says that if the house is swept clean and left empty, it becomes subject to the invasion of even more evil spirits (Matthew 12:43–45). So unless Vicky accepts Jesus as Lord, so that the Holy Spirit fills their place, she would be in that situation, wouldn't she?'

'That's true,' he agreed. 'If an unbeliever is possessed by evil spirits, it would be much better to bind them and cut the person concerned off from their influence, so that they are set free to choose whether or not they want to follow Jesus.'

As the days progressed, Vicky became more and more unsettled, slipping out of the house, ostensibly for a walk, and often not returning until late in the evening.

'I can't help it, Mum,' she complained tearfully. 'I'm lonely without my friends around me. I know you and Peter mean well, but you're older than me, and Ruth and Sarah don't do the things I want to do.'

It was hardly surprising. What Vicky wanted to do was to go to the pub as often as possible, and there to drink as much as she could.

'You know where she's going, I suppose?' Peter asked, naming the most notorious place in town. 'How long do you suppose it'll be before she gets hold of more drugs?'

'Oh, surely not?' I replied naïvely. 'She's so determined to come off.'

Nevertheless, I remonstrated with Vicky herself. 'Oh, Mum!' she cried. 'Stop worrying. I'm only having a bit of fun.'

A couple of days later, as if to prove her point, she told me of some 'guy' who had offered her cocaine. 'But you see,' she spread her hands upward, 'I didn't take it.'

'Why should they offer it to her?' I asked Peter.

'Well, it's obvious to anyone what she is,' he replied.

Vicky began arriving home with strange young men, usually leather clad, tattooed and earringed.

'It may not be a very Christian way of looking at things,' Peter remarked, 'but it makes me feel very uneasy having all these strange bods in the house. I find myself wondering all the time if they're "casing the joint".'

'I thought you'd be pleased that someone walks me home,' Vicky protested.

One evening she did not appear at all. 'I'd better get the car out and go looking for her,' Peter said in concern. Images of her lying doped or dead in a doorway filled my mind as Peter scoured the town. In the event, she arrived home on foot in the early hours with yet another young man.

In the effort to distract her, to fill her empty days, I encouraged Vicky to use her artistic gifts. Weird drawings began to fill the sketch book I gave her, depicting creatures with strange demonic faces, a look of evil in their eyes. Always she was the victim of their menacing attentions, while in another graphic drawing she showed herself falling from a cloud into a bottomless pit as the world spun merrily on its way.

Christian friends, lunching with us one day, called our attention to writing on Vicky's window, evidently inscribed sometime previously, but now revealed in the condensation on the glass. 'I hate Victoria' it read, and elsewhere were written equally disturbing self-revelations. 'She's obviously in torment,' our friends sympathized, offering their help in any way possible.

In the event, there was nothing anyone could do. Receiving a telephone call one afternoon, Vicky suddenly announced her intention of leaving, telling me only that Melanie, her old college friend, was in need of help.

12

Within His Reach

As well as the vision the Lord had given me to sustain me through this hour of need, there were also Bible verses which had spoken to me. How often we feel as mothers, that no one can love, understand or yearn after our children's well-being as we can. For those of us who have known the anguish of single-parenthood, the problem is intensified. Can God really be trusted to care for our offspring as we do ourselves?

As Vicky disappeared from the scene once more, I was reminded of a verse which the Lord had given me soon after my divorce, and remembered anew that my daughter was his creation, and only mine by deed of gift. From his holy dwelling, God is 'father to the fatherless' (Psalm 68:5). 'And that, my child,' I seemed to hear him say, 'means that however great your love and concern, mine is far greater.'

'But Lord,' I prayed, 'how can we ever bring Vicky through this if she keeps disappearing? How can she ever come to know you if she keeps going back to the drug scene? What hope is there of her giving her life to you when she's surrounded by other addicts?' 'Is the Lord's arm too short?' I read in my Bible (Numbers 11:23). How foolish I was to suppose that the Lord could not act without me, nor reach Vicky when she was

146

out of my reach.

With news of Vicky's return to London, and her old way of life, I began praying with friends that God would not let her go but would in some way bring her back once more. On a Friday morning in March, my Bible reading further enforced the goodness of God: 'Not one of all the Lord's good promises to the house of Israel failed; every one was fulfilled' (Joshua 21:45). Since many of the other promises I had received following my divorce had reached fruition, there remained only the vision outstanding. Was the Lord telling me that this was about to be fulfilled? How would he go about it? In what way would he so arrange the circumstances of life so as to bring it about? A great air of expectation filled me.

When Jim rang later in the morning to tell me of the death of his mother the previous night after a chronic condition, though saddened for him in his loss, it seemed to me that this might have some part to play. Vicky obviously had to be informed, and Jim made this a matter for personal attention. 'You see, my child,' I seemed to hear the Lord saying, 'no one is beyond my reach. Though far from you, my arm is not too short to touch the lives of those I love.'

Nothing less, I was sure, would have brought Vicky home again at that time. The Lord had used the demise of her grandmother, and the funeral a week later, to confront her with the reality of death in the midst of life. In hearing the ancient words of Scripture, Vicky could hardly fail to realize the gravity of her own situation.

Her visit was brief. Arriving just in time for the short service at the crematorium, she announced her intention of returning to London immediately after, despite the distances involved and the pleas of her father and me. Was I wrong? Was her heart so hardened that nothing could touch it?

My eyes filled with tears. She looked ill, her mouth covered in herpes, and a hacking cough coming from her thin body. Guessing that her next fix was her most immediate requirement, I drove her to the station, silently pleading with the Lord to move upon her. As she turned to say goodbye, prior to boarding the train, her plea for help once again finally came. The Lord's arm had proved not to be too short.

There had been no previous experience among the ministers and elders of our church in dealing with drug addiction, and therefore little knowledge of where one could go for help and advice. Through various means I was put in touch with different agencies, including some Christian hostels, but Vicky refused to consider any long-term rehabilitation. Her aim was to come home once more, come off the drugs as quickly as possible, and resume her old way of life. No amount of persuasion on my part could convince her otherwise.

'As far as I can see, she needs a complete change of lifestyle,' I said to her father during an ensuing telephone conversation. 'She needs to be like a reformed alcoholic and stay out of temptation's way. Going back to the same friends and environment isn't going to work.'

'I don't altogether agree,' he said, laughing cynically at my analogy, 'just let's get her off the stuff without worrying about the future.'

His opinion seemed also to be shared by some of the literature I had received. Families Anonymous had sent a card, among the lists of addresses for self-help groups, stating quasi-Christian attitudes to be fostered in those seeking to help drug abusers. One of them declared: 'I will have no thought for the future actions of others, neither expecting them to be better or worse as time goes on, for in such expectations I am really trying to create. I will love and let be.' It finished: 'I can change myself. Others I can only love.' On a smaller card, the 'serenity prayer' was printed.

SCODA (the Standing Conference On Drug Abuse) had sent other helpful literature with lists of rehabilitation centres, giving information on drug abuse, (including some of the jargon and slang names for opiates and barbiturates), withdrawal (or detoxification) and treatment, as well as a statement on the Home Office Index. From the Blenheim Project I received two practical guides, one for the addict, the other for relatives and friends. Vicky too had procured similar leaflets and booklets, and I was encouraged, as she returned home once more, to see that she was making an effort at self-help.

'Will you think about coming off cold?' I asked as we settled her into her old bedroom. 'We could arrange round-the-clock prayer for you.' Already she was being prayed for regularly on our prayer-chain, and in the prayer triplets meetings in the run-up to Billy Graham's visit, but unable to face up to the pain and discomfort she was convinced she would experience, Vicky begged me to find some other way.

Through my GP arrangements were made for Vicky to see a psychiatrist, Dr Byron, prior to admission to hospital. 'We will not administer methadone unless you're under supervision,' he told Vicky, splaying his pudgy fingers on the desk-top. 'It will mean going into the admissions ward of the psychiatric hospital. We don't have any other facilities in the county, and there are only two beds there. I have telephoned and they have one available this afternoon.'

Shock registered on Vicky's face. It obviously wasn't going to be as easy as she'd at first envisaged. Though I would still have preferred her to accept prayer help at home, to me it seemed like a miracle that one of only two beds should be available so readily.

'Society makes no provision for people like me,' she cried bitterly as we left. 'Two beds in the county! That's pathetic!'

'Well, Vicky,' I said softly, as we walked towards the carpark, 'I suppose there are so many sick people need-ing beds in hospitals, they don't look kindly on those whom they consider inflict their sickness on themselves.'

Vicky swung her shoulder-bag violently through the air. 'It's society's problem and society ought to b***** well do something about it!' she cried.

'Vicky!' I retorted, reacting to her language. 'You can't go through the rest of your life expecting a living from society when you've put nothing into it yourself.'

'It's all very well,' she yanked at the car door and threw herself into the passenger seat as I started the engine, 'but even the law protects those bringing dope into the country. I know of diplomats who come to our club and boast about bringing the stuff through customs in their luggage. Because of diplomatic immunity, no one can touch them. They're stinking rich, laden with gold and diamond jewellery—all made out of drug-running.'

It was strange, I reflected, how lucid she became when on her high horse, the slovenly accent forgotten. Strange, too, how these nameless diplomats could incite her anger, while the Patti's of this world, though equally intent on getting their cut, were seen to be benefactors in providing for her needs. Still, I couldn't stay angry with her for long. The tensions which had begun in Dr Byron's office built up throughout lunch-time, so that as the time to leave for the psychiatric unit approached, Vicky was in a high old state.

'I can't go through with it Mum,' she said in a hoarse whisper as she smoked one cigarette after another.

'What's the alternative, darling?' I put my hand on her knee, smiling ruefully. 'You won't come off cold here; you won't spend a year in a rehabilitation centre; this is all that's left.'

The hospital was large and Victorian, a formidable building though set in beautiful grounds.

'It won't be so bad,' I said as we made our way up the long drive, but it was as much to reassure myself as her. An old man shuffled towards me as we walked to the enquiry office, spittle forming bubbles around his lips and dribbling down the unshaven chin. Repeatedly aiming an unintelligible question at me, he followed in our wake. Aware of Vicky's reaction, I forced myself to smile brightly and pass the time of day with him.

'Take me home, Mum. Take me home. I can't stay

here. I can't.' Back in the sanctuary of the car once more, Vicky broke down in tears.

'Darling, you're not even going to be in this part of the hospital. We've got to drive round to the back. And that old man isn't to be feared.' Deliberately keeping my voice cheerful, I started the engine.

Nevertheless, I had to admit to an overwhelming feeling of depression as we found the admissions ward. It was quite unlike any conventional hospital, the day-rooms and dining-room having a general air of dirt and neglect. The stale smell of food lingered in the air, mingling with the inevitable tobacco smoke. I wrinkled my nose, noting the grubby peeling paint and nicotine-stained ceilings.

'This ward is not for the really mentally sick,' a nurse explained. 'We take in anorexics, people suffering acute depression, that sort of thing.'

'What an appalling place to put anyone suffering depression,' I said quietly to the charge nurse as Vicky was ushered ahead of me down a long dark corridor. 'I should think this must entrench them in their despair and despondency.'

'What about us?' he said sardonically, side-stepping a middle-aged woman who lay on the floor, a glazed expression on her face as she muttered unintelligibly to the ceiling. 'We have to put up with it year in and year out.'

'Could God possibly be present in a place like this?' I wondered.

Vicky, still filled with apprehension, was thoroughly uncommunicative, refusing to be drawn into answering anything more than monosyllabically, as a young trainee nurse sought to question her on her background and feelings.

'What does any of that matter? All I want is to get off smack and get out of here as soon as possible,' she cried, casting her eyes fearfully at the other patients. Sudden enlightenment dawned on me. She was seeing herself, for the first time, as she believed others saw her—an 'outcast' from society, a social leper, someone to be 'shut away' from 'normal, decent folk'.

A timid little woman approached me as we left the nurse and made our way towards the day-room. Her clothes hung on her meagre frame as on a wooden clothes-horse, her feet thrust into carpet slippers. She engaged me in conversation, having a benign smile on her face and a seemingly childlike desire for my attention as she clutched my arm. I seated myself beside her, and since talk turned easily that way, began to speak to her of the Lord Jesus. Soon another came over, a lady with Parkinson's disease, her voice as trembly as her hands. The more folk I spoke with, the easier it became.

To begin with, my motives were mixed. If Vicky could see me reacting normally to those she considered abnormal, then perhaps her fear of the unknown might be dissolved. Surprisingly, however—at least to me—it was my own fear which began to vanish, to be replaced by a genuine compassion for these folk. I felt that the Lord was giving me new eyes to see and a new heart to love them as he did.

After several hours, during which I managed to disengage myself long enough to chat with Vicky, I left to go home, promising to return next day. It was a long journey and my heart was heavy, my eyes misting with unshed tears as I thought of her alone in that place.

'It's painful, Lord, seeing your loved ones suffering, even when it's been brought about in this way. I hate leaving her there in that awful place. Be with her, Lord Jesus, and use this experience to bring her to that point of need where she knows only you are the answer.'

Everything in me had cried out to bring her home with me as we'd parted. But love has to be tough—tough enough not to give in to the easy way out. For the umpteenth time, as a parent, I caught a glimpse of that parental love with which the Lord loves us—its strength, its sorrow, its pain.

My daily visits occupied all my free time. Vicky continued to be uncommunicative, becoming more and

more difficult so that eventually, after being caught
sneaking off the premises and down to the local pub, she
was made to sign a form and forbidden to leave the
ward. Constantly sick and suffering withdrawal symptoms with the reducing dose of methadone, she became
increasingly abusive with what she saw as the staff's lack
of concern, thus alienating them still further.

'I can't go on, Mum,' she wept. 'I can't stay here any
longer. I might as well give up now. They just hate me
here, and I hate them.'

This, it seemed to me, was the root problem. These
feelings of rejection, of being hated and of hating in
turn, had been present in her from an early age, domin-
ating every relationship and experience throughout her
school-days. She seemed willing to listen as I spelled out
all that the Lord could do for her, and though there was
no glimmer of acceptance on her part, she was more
open with me than she had ever been. She also seemed
to have some sort of understanding of what she had put
me through. As she related the story of a friend in
London who had been imprisoned for a drugs offence,
she told me of the concern and grief this had caused the
girl's parents. 'I felt really sorry for them,' she said. 'I
can see now what you went through. Her mum always
prays for me, and had her whole church praying, like
you did.' I wondered if this could be a further instance
of the Lord reaching out to her.

One evening, nearly a fortnight after she had first
been admitted, I told Vicky I would be unable to visit the
next day. 'It's your grandfather's seventieth birthday
tomorrow,' I said, 'and I'd like to be there. But your
father has asked if he might be allowed to come to see
you.'

Because of Vicky's lack of co-operation, she had been
barred from having any visitors save myself. I'd explained the situation to Jim and he had made arrangements with the staff to visit on the day of the party.

The birthday party went off well, and was a pleasant
oasis for me, steeped as I had been in the depressing

circumstances of the hospital. We'd travelled home from my parents afterwards, in time to make it to the evening service at church.

It was as I was preparing to visit Vicky the following day that I received a telephone call from the hospital.

'I did try to reach you yesterday,' the charge nurse began. 'We've had complaints from another patient who says that Victoria borrowed money from him when she discharged herself yesterday. He's worried about how it will be repaid.'

'Discharged herself?' My mind was frantically trying to piece together all that he had left unsaid. 'What do you mean? Has Vicky left?'

It transpired that Jim had not arrived to see her after all. Vicky had, therefore, telephoned friends some forty or fifty miles away and asked them to visit her. This was precisely what the hospital staff had been trying to avoid, and back in the company of her old gang, she had been enticed into leaving the hated discipline and strictures of the ward for the more libertine pleasures beckoning beyond.

Quite apart from the fact that Vicky was prepared to have me travel all those miles before discovering her absence (which I would have done, had not one of the patients complained), I had to face up to the fact that she seemed to want freedom from her addiction only if it could be achieved at minimal cost to her lifestyle. Until such times as she really meant business, there seemed little that anyone could do. And yet . . . we had seemed so nearly there.

During the ensuing days, there was the temptation of thinking, 'If only. . . .' If only Jim had kept his promise; if only her friends had been unavailable; and most poignant of all, if only I'd spent the day with Vicky as usual. Perhaps six months previously, I might have succumbed to that temptation, but God was now to show me that he is to be trusted.

Within days of Vicky's disappearance, some verses from Isaiah were added to my storehouse of promises:

'Enlarge the place of your tent, stretch your tent curtains wide, do not hold back; lengthen your cords,
strengthen your stakes. For you will spread out to the
right and to the left; *your descendants will dispossess
nations and settle in their desolate cities*' (Isaiah 54:2–3,
my italics). My vision had been too small. I was to look
beyond my own limited parameters to the wonderful
resources of a God who knows no bounds. My faith was
to be strengthened, staked in the unshakable Rock, so
that no matter how much the Enemy might seek to destroy, my tent would hold firm.

As I read on, I saw that the Lord was showing me the
way he had already led me, as if to remind me that he
had never let me down. It was as if the verses had been
written for me alone, speaking of 'a wife deserted and
distressed in spirit—a wife who married young, only to
be rejected' (Isaiah 54:6), and continuing with what the
Lord had done for me: 'With deep compassion I will
bring you back.' And he had! How he had blessed me—
with healing, both physical and spiritual, making me
whole in Christ; in my marriage to Peter, restoring a
family life for Sarah and Ruth. Promises followed of the
way the Lord would build me up 'with stones of tur-
quoise . . . foundations with sapphires . . . battlements of
rubies' (Isaiah 54:11–12). And finally, for my children:
'All your sons [daughters] will be taught by the Lord,
and great will be your children's peace' (Isaiah 54:13).

I was yet to discover the way in which those promises
were to begin their fulfilment.

13

A Heroin Heaven?

Soon after Vicky's departure from the psychiatric hospital, Jim rang to say that he had heard from her. A violent disagreement had ensued between us, leaving me shaking and distressed. Vicky seemed to be setting us off one against the other. She had asked me, while still in the hospital, to enlist her father's support in helping her in a business venture. Subsequently she had approached him herself, and he now made it clear that he expected me to finance a partnership between Melanie, her common-law husband, and Vicky herself. Needless to say, I did not feel that this was a satisfactory solution to Vicky's problems.

But if I'd had any lingering doubts as to whether God's promises were to be trusted, they were soon to be dispelled. Prayer for Vicky continued in our prayer triplets, that somehow she would be reached. I now saw the problem in a new light. Ceasing to ask for her well-being —though not for her ultimate protection—I asked that she might know no peace until she surrendered.

'Don't let anything in her life become comfortable to her, Lord,' I prayed. 'Make it so miserable that she has to turn to you.'

Throughout the spring we prayed, and as the summer began the second part of God's promise began to unfold. Ruth—my quiet, thoughtful youngest daughter—gave her heart to the Lord in the most public way imaginable. Making three one-hundred-mile trips to the nearest Billy Graham rally, while I was in hospital recovering from an operation, she went forward with hundreds of others to make her commitment. My joy knew no bounds.

'Actually, I gave my heart to the Lord about eighteen months ago, just before we moved,' she admitted shyly. 'But that was in private. I knew I had to make a public commitment.'

Knowing her diffidence, despite her seventeen years, it was easy to appreciate the courage such a step had taken. If the Lord could do it for her he could do it for anyone. The vision was coming to fruition. Both Sarah and Ruth had been in his net, and were now in the palm of his hand.

'I didn't notice in the vision, and often wondered the order in which they'd come,' I confided to a friend. 'But with Sarah having rededicated her life three years ago at Hildenborough, and now Ruth—well, there's only Vicky left isn't there?'

The summer came and went, and with it Vicky's twenty-first birthday. My heart was heavy with the passing of what should have been so happy an occasion. Then, one day shortly afterwards, in the middle of the afternoon, Vicky rang long-distance from London. She was in obvious distress, but brushing my concern aside, asked me instead to speak to her friend Tina.

Having learned from Vicky on previous occasions the nature of this woman's livelihood, I could imagine little that she would have to say which would be of interest to me. A prostitute in Soho, she had borne several children by different fathers and had recently been imprisoned for possessing drugs, though Vicky assured me she was now 'straight' in that respect at least.

'Vicky's afraid to speak to you herself,' she began,' and too ashamed to ask you for help again. She's back on the drugs, but if you could have her home to get her off again, I'll look after her once she's clear.'

I could feel myself bristling. How could it possibly be glorifying to God to liaise with this woman? What sort of 'looking after' would Vicky receive from her hand? I'd said it before, and I'd say it again: Until such time as Vicky turned her back on the whole scene, renouncing all her old friends and haunts, she'd never get anywhere. Others may conquer their drug addiction without knowing Jesus; for Vicky that could never be. The more I'd considered the question, the more I believed that nothing less than her commitment to the Lord would effect any lasting change in her lifestyle.

'Would you put Vicky back on please?' I said aloud, and as she passed the receiver over, 'We'll help you again, Vicky, but not for you to go back there. You have to make up your mind to begin a new life.'

'Oh yes, Mum,' Vicky said with obvious relief, 'I really will this time.' She paused. 'I've just come out of hospital.' Her voice broke and I knew she was crying. 'I overdosed. Oh Mum, I'm so afraid. One of my friends died.' I heard her sharp intake of breath as my heart missed a beat.

It was only as I went to bed that night and re-read my Bible notes from the morning reading, that the significance of what had happened really sank in. I read: 'Our spiritual progress is determined by our view of God. If we hold a limited or inadequate picture of him, this will mirror itself in how we live and what we ask of him. He is not just mighty, but Almighty!' (Selwyn Hughes, *Every Day with Jesus* (Crusade for World Revival)). I copied it into my diary. My view of God had enlarged. The verses from Isaiah had caused me to look upwards and outwards as I'd enlarged the place of my tent. And as I did so the vastness of this Almighty God had been stretched before me.

Hadn't he done just what I'd asked and not given Vicky any peace? He was letting her know real fear. As she witnessed the death of her friend through overdosing, the realization of her own gamble with life was vividly portrayed. The horror of his corpse, lying crumpled and ravaged in a doorway, the punctured limbs and tortured body stiffening into rigor mortis, could not easily be forgotten by one who had herself been so close to that pitiable state. Vicky could hardly fail to be aware of the fact that she herself had been within a hair's breadth of so ignominious a death. Yet God had demonstrated his power and his faithfulness in not letting her go; in protecting her at the last.

Turning to switch out the bedside lamp, I settled down for the night, still filled with the wonder of what had happened. The Lord's timing was perfect. Though brought up in the Anglican church, we were now attending a large baptist fellowship and Ruth had decided to be baptized. That happy event was scheduled for the end of the week. Vicky would thus be at home to witness her sister's declaration of the Lordship of Jesus in her life.

'Thank you, Lord,' I murmured, before drifting into sleep.

It would appear that the significance of these events had not passed the notice of the devil either, and as I collected Vicky for the third time from the bus depot, it was evident that he was out to do all in his power to make life difficult.

Vicky had decided, on this occasion, to come off 'cold turkey'. As she stumbled from the bus, however, it was obvious to all that she was as high as a kite; so drugged up that she couldn't even stand. Sliding an arm around her waist to support her, I found it difficult to control the tears. Her condition had deteriorated markedly, her faculties completely under the domination of evil. Somehow I managed to stow her and the inevitable plastic carrier-bags containing her meagre possessions into the car. She flopped like a rag-doll against the seat, her head lolling and eyes rolling upwards. Her speech was slurred and laborious, as if the English language had suddenly become a foreign tongue.

'Why is it Lord, that each time I think I can be hurt

and distressed no more, I'm proved wrong? Will it ever get any easier?' Into my mind flashed the thought that this is how it is at all times for the Lord, as he grieves for his fallen creation.

Summoning the strength of will from somewhere, as we drew up outside the house, Vicky managed to lever herself from the car, staggering drunkenly, and collapsing abruptly into a small untidy heap on the pavement. She giggled foolishly. A fleeting thought went through my head as to what the neighbours would make of all this, but I was beyond caring. All that mattered was to free my daughter from the bondage of such degradation.

It didn't take long to find out why Vicky was as she was. Determined to take no more heroin, she had sought to hedge off the worst of the withdrawal symptoms, so she believed, by stuffing herself full of various other drugs. Armed with a MIMS (Monthly Index of Medical Specialities) directory, no doubt stolen from some chemist shop, she had acquired a staggering knowledge of the names, nature and derivatives of most of its contents.

Still very much under the influence of her drug cocktail, and unable to control her limbs, Vicky produced handfuls of small polythene bags filled with brightly coloured pills.

'Here,' she thrust them into Peter's hands as soon as he appeared home from work. 'Take these please, and don't let me have them back no matter what,' she mumbled.

As soon as he was able, without her knowledge, Peter took them to our pharmacist friend for analysis.

'This is how they're packaged by the drug companies for sending out to the chemist,' he explained, turning the vividly hued packets over in his hands and naming them as nembutal, diazepine and vallium. 'They're undoubtedly black market and extremely dangerous in these quantities. I'm not surprised she couldn't stand. Three of these in a day is the normal dose.'

Vicky, I knew, had been taking far in excess of that,

but as she explained, 'I'm not normal.' I could appreciate that when you'd been on heroin as long as she had, the effectiveness of any drug must be diminished. But I also knew, from the literature I'd received last time she was home, that the barbiturates could be more dangerous during detoxification than the opiates. Her pills might help to calm her down while she was taking them, but withdrawal would be even harder than from heroin.

So it proved. During the next forty-eight hours Vicky evidently lived through hell, and it was not far short of that for us. She rolled on the floor crying in agony, the sobs rasping in her throat as she clutched at the cramps in her stomach. At other times it would be her legs which were most affected, and though I prayed aloud with her, nothing seemed to avail. 'Perhaps she has to go through all this to ensure that she'll never go back on heroin again,' I thought. But my anguish grew by the hour, especially when I found Ruth weeping quietly in her room, her head covered by a pillow, unable to bear the sight and sound of her sister's torment any longer.

'Give me my pills,' Vicky screamed intermittently, threatening to take a carving knife to Peter if he did not comply. The sense of impotence grew within me, and I knew that without his resolute refusal, I would have weakened.

'Please help me, Mum, please help me. Get the doctor.' It was more than I could endure. Reaching for the telephone, I rang the surgery.

'I'm sorry Mrs Scott,' his voice came briskly down the line. 'Your daughter's had her chance. We only have two beds. It wouldn't be fair to deprive some other person. Tell her to go back to London.'

'To what?' I thought. Ultimately to certain death.

The rule on no smoking was forgotten in the trauma of the ensuing days and nights. We were in constant fear of Vicky setting the house on fire, and prayed 'without ceasing', binding the Enemy so that he might be made impotent. The realities of spiritual warfare were with us all continually as we battled night and day, engaging in mortal combat with an enemy who clearly did not want to lose one of his prize possessions, as he must have thought. It left us all drained and tense, exhausted beyond measure, irritable and strained, despite the prayer ministry of others.

Vicky developed a craving for sugary foods, raiding the freezer as she had before. I would find her, in the morning surrounded by evidence of her forays, ice-cream, chocolate cakes and the like smeared into her bedding and night clothes. Gone was any remnant of decency—she became like an animal, caged in with its own filth. The subtlety of the wolf in sheep's clothing—the devil who offered a free trip to a heroin heaven—was revealed in all his starkness as a lion roaring in anger, showing himself for what he really was. Evil so corrupt, so vile and so shameful was hard to imagine. But Satan had been disclosed—his burning desire to assail the nostrils of the Almighty and pollute the sweet fragrance of paradise.

Not for the first time, I recalled the trappings of witchcraft and pagan idolatry which Vicky had brought back from Nigeria and wondered just what her involvement had been—if at all. Ouija boards, too, had been in evidence at the convent according to Sarah, though she herself had never used them. But Vicky? She was an unknown quantity. Was there some occult influence which my friend's cousin had seen in Vicky all those years ago when he'd spoken of her having a 'mouthful of threepenny bits'?

One day, after lunch, I went up to where Vicky lay in squalor on her bed. For some time we talked, trying to make sense of it all, our frayed nerves serving only to lead us into an ever increasing maze of uncertainty and distress as our voices rose. Then, for a moment we sat in silence, each nursing our secret thoughts and fears. Suddenly rousing herself, Vicky shrieked, 'You might as well forget me.' The tears coursing down her face left blackened trails of mascara as she huddled in a foetal position on the mattress. 'I'm never going to be anything but a junkie till the day I die,' she continued, her face, blotchy with crying, half hidden in the duvet.

'How can I forget you?' I cried, weeping profusely. 'I love you.' I shouted, raising my head to hurl the words across the room at her. 'You're asking the impossible. You can't just switch off loving someone.'

Through the open window the lazy sounds of summer drifted upwards: Peter and Ruth sharing a conversation in hushed and murmuring tones as they sipped their coffee in the garden below; a neighbour's radio playing softly as she lay basking in the heat of the sun.

I crossed the room, sitting on the end of Vicky's bed and stroked her matted hair. 'I can't just cut you out of my heart, Vicky. It doesn't work like that.' The tears still flowing, my raised voice was husky with emotion as I continued. 'But you don't have to be a junkie for the rest of your life. You can choose. If you choose to follow Jesus, he'll make you a new creation. You can be enslaved to him, so that he has control of your life.' I paused, my voice dropping a tone. 'Or you can choose to be enslaved to sin, so that heroin has control of you,' I finished.

'I can't do anything while I'm in this pain.' She stuffed a corner of the duvet into her mouth to stifle the sobs, her thin body writhing on the bed. 'Please ask the doctor for help again, Mum, please.'

Such are the wiles of the devil. Better by far for him to relinquish, momentarily, his hold on a person in order to fool them into thinking they have victory. Off the drugs and out of pain—then she'll be free to choose goes his reasoning. Thus can he 'save' them from the ultimate victory of new life in Christ. And he took me in. Unable to bear for a moment longer the anguish of my daughter, I telephoned the psychiatrist direct and begged him for help, despite the refusal of my GP. To my tired mind, clouded by emotion, it was only in hindsight that I could see that introducing a human agent once more provided an escape route for Vicky to bypass Jesus.

I still had a lot to learn. As Vicky sat in the psychiatrist's office once more, it was a relief to hear that he would agree to put her on a reducing dose of methadone as a day-patient. She was to report daily to the hospital for a twenty-four hour dosage. There was one proviso, and that was that she was to attend weekly at a session of Narcotics Anonymous.

'And just see that you pull yourself together,' he admonished scathingly as the visit was concluded. 'How much longer do you think you can keep coming crying to Mummy? It's about time, at your age, that you took some responsibility for your own life.'

Ruth's baptism took place on the Sunday evening of the following week, and Vicky, by this time, was well enough to attend. It was one more witness to her, in a packed church of five or six hundred people, as to the reality of Jesus.

Shortly before the half-dozen or so candidates came forward one by one, I distinctly saw a vision of Vicky, dressed in white, going down under the water. It was so real that I was quite taken aback and had to blink hard. Though there was no outward sign afterwards of the experience having made any impression on her at all, I took this as a prophetic word from the Lord as to his plans for the future.

'Two down and one to go,' I thought remembering the vision of the water's edge.

14

'All This Jesus Business'

'I don't know why you keep feeling it has to be your way,' Vicky said crossly, eyeing me from the bed where she sat, knees in the air, back resting on the wall. 'I know lots of junkies who've kicked the habit without all this Jesus business.'

It was now only a fortnight since she had been put on an eight-week reduction course of methadone, yet already Vicky had reduced the dose so rapidly as to be nearly off altogether. The colour was returning to her cheeks, and her eyes had lost the dulled and glazed appearance so typical of the addict.

She still spent a considerable amount of time alone in her room, despite my hope that she would become more integrated into family life. But with her mind cleared of the drug-crazed influences of heroin and barbiturates, she had become more lucid in her thinking, expressing truths I had hitherto only been able to guess at. And this was one of those rare gems.

'I'm sure there may well be those who come off drugs without a Christian faith,' I agreed, sitting on the spare bed and regarding my daughter across the room. 'But it isn't *my* way Vicky, its God's. The Bible says that Jesus is the *only* way (John 14:6). You've known all about Jesus ever since you were a little girl.'

165

I hesitated, wondering how far to go, then clasping my hands in my lap, continued: 'The Lord had shown me that he won't be content until you give your life to him. He loves you too much to let you go.'

'I do believe in God,' she furrowed her brow in concentration, picking absent-mindedly at a piece of thread in the new jeans I had bought her. 'And I pray to him when I need to. But it's just all this churchy, Jesus-loves-you, lovey-dovey rubbish. I'm young. Can't you understand that, Mum?' The tears began to form. 'I just want to have *fun*.'

'Darling you can have fun,' I replied earnestly. 'But being hooked on heroin isn't much fun, is it?' I paused, allowing the remark to sink in, then continued. 'Anyway, going back to what you were saying earlier, being a Christian isn't just a matter of believing in God in the sense of believing in his existence. It means believing in the sense of trusting yourself to him.' I leaned forwards, pressing home the message. 'You can believe that a number thirty-seven bus goes to town, but unless you get on it and trust that it will take you to town, you won't actually get there.'

'Well quite honestly, I think you're all hypocrites.' Vicky rose abruptly from her semi-reclining position on the bed, swinging her legs to the ground and perching on the edge. 'There you were, all those years, talking about Jesus this and Jesus that, going to church, reading your Bible and praying, but what sort of life did we get? All you and Dad did was row, row, row.'

I thought, 'We've had this conversation before.' Aloud I said, 'Yes, Vicky. I know there were rows. Your father and I were constantly pulling in different directions. All I ever wanted for you girls was that you should have a happy home life. But there were things your father wanted to do which I just couldn't go along with.'

'Well it didn't work out like that, did it?' Vicky's head came up accusingly. 'It was awful. I hated it. I started on drugs when I was fourteen just to have some sort of escape.'

Fourteen! Why, she was still at the convent then!

'It was only soft drugs to begin with,' she continued. 'It was quite easy to get them at school. The day-girls had access to any amount. You remember that time I was nearly expelled for smoking? The nuns didn't even realize what it was.'

'Was it so dreadful, Vicky? That must have been after your father and I split up.'

'Yes. But it was awful before that. It was the rows that did it.'

'Vicky, I'm sorry.' My voice faltered. 'I'm so sorry, darling. You do know, don't you, that your father had . . . affairs.' She nodded. 'I was devastated. It was as if the bottom had dropped out of my world. I know I didn't cope well, even though I was a Christian. But if I hadn't been one, I wouldn't have coped at all.'

'Yes, well you were always saying how like Dad I was. You didn't get on with him and ended up getting divorced, so you must have felt the same for me.' Her face was set in hard lines as if determined not to give in to the emotion within, and she shrugged one shoulder as if to deny the importance of her statement.

Ironically, it was something I had always tried to avoid doing—making unfavourable comparisons, yet I had to admit that the temptation is ever present. How many parents can honestly say that they have never renounced their offspring's worst traits, attributing them to the other parent, while claiming credit for the good themselves? How easy it is to retort 'just like your father' whenever some irritation occurs. Yet what more could I do than apologize if I had indeed succumbed and wounded her?

I crossed the room and crouched by Vicky's bed, taking her hand in mine. 'Vicky, please forgive me for all the hurt that's been inflicted on you by my selfishness, my bad parenting, my preoccupation with self.'

All the things which the Lord had revealed to me three years earlier when I'd prayed for healing for the three girls, flooded back. 'She needs to know that you accept your part,' I seemed to hear the Lord saying.

'Oh, Mum,' Vicky pulled her hand away, bursting into tears. 'For goodness' sake.' Her voice rose. 'There's no one to blame but myself. I was the one who decided to take drugs. I'm responsible for my own actions.' She rose and crossed the room, leaning her forehead against the window to gaze unseeingly to the garden below.

'I always had Sarah thrown at me at school,' she continued bleakly. '"Why can't you be more like your sister?" That's what they kept saying. She was such a goody-goody, I wanted to be different. I wanted to be me. I wanted to be a person in my own right.' Her voice took on an impassioned tone. 'I've got a personality—a jolly sight more than Sarah. But all I ever got was her being thrust down my throat.'

Angrily she dashed the tears from her eyes. 'I hated our way of life too. They were all such snobs at school. I wanted to be different. I hated it when Dad took us back on Mondays, because it was always in the big car. You're all just hypocrites. Where do all the poor people fit into your religion?'

All this hatred inside, I thought. And all the rejection —the lack of acceptance of herself. She'd wanted to be different. But at what cost?

'When I first started with soft drugs, I felt I was in control. I wanted to punish you and Dad for all the misery.' Vicky turned from the window, leaning back against the sill. 'Later, I wanted my problems to force you and Dad together again. Patti supplied all I needed.' Her voice broke as she continued. 'But, of course, eventually the drugs controlled me. Sometimes I wonder if I'll ever really be free.'

A shaft of sunlight, slanting into the room, lit up Vicky's face, bringing some semblance of youth and beauty to the downcast features.

'When Gerald came over the other day, darling,' I said, in reference to the visit of one of our church elders, 'he prayed that you would be loosed from the influence of the drugs, cut off from their power. That means that you're free. Do you understand what that means?'

Vicky shook her head a trifle impatiently, and bending her knees, squatted on the floor, leaning back against the radiator beneath the window.

'You remember we've talked before about being free?' I leaned forwards, resting my forearms on my knees. 'Well, in a book I've been reading, there's a story of two men. Every morning they walked to work together, and every morning one of them bought a newspaper from a newsagent. The vendor was always extremely rude, but the man buying the paper never got ruffled at all. He was always as courteous and polite as could be. One day his friend asked why he remained so nice to the ill-mannered news-vendor. "Because I don't want *him* to decide how *I'm* going to act," the man replied.' (John Powell, *Why Am I Afraid to Tell You Who I Am?* [Fontana/Collins]). I straightened up, and paused for effect. 'Do you see, Vicky? You can choose how you want to behave. You don't have to allow other people, or circumstances, to dictate to you the sort of person you are.'

Vicky sighed, a pained expression on her face. 'I don't suppose he came from a broken home,' she replied.

'That doesn't matter, love. You have a straight choice. You can say to yourself: "I come from a broken home, therefore life has dealt me a rotten hand and everything I do from now on will be influenced by my past. I have no control over that. It will pull me down, no matter what." That way you can wallow in self-pity, believing that the world owes you something from life.'

Crossing one leg over the other, I leaned back on one arm before continuing. 'Or you can tell yourself that despite having come from a broken home, you are going to overcome any disadvantage. Use those experiences as a launch pad to greater things. Better still, let God use them. The Bible says that God "comforts us in all our troubles, so that we can comfort those in any trouble with the comfort we ourselves have received from God" (2 Corinthians 1:4).

'I have thought about helping other addicts. Oh, don't

worry,' Vicky's head came up defensively, 'not until I'm completely over it myself. But seeing how little understanding there is in the medical profession has made me realize that only an ex-addict can help someone with a habit, because only they know what it's like to be dependent.'

'Well that's a good step forward,' I said, glad of her perception and progress yet aware of a certain need for caution. Could this be a light at the end of the tunnel? A new hope fo the future?

'For instance,' Vicky continued more brightly, 'did you know that when you're on heroin, your endorphins stop working? Endorphins are what stop you feeling pain, so when you come off the drugs that's why you get the cramps. Eating sugar helps restore the body's natural balance.'

I wondered, in the days that followed, how much of this information and more positive thinking was attributable to Narcotics Anonymous. Vicky had attended regularly on the three Mondays since seeing Dr Byron, but a certain coyness was evident in her demeanour about the content of the sessions. There had been a marked degree of reluctance as she'd flashed some literature before my eyes when I'd made enquiry, and it was some weeks before I was able to see for myself wherein lay their success.

The Twelve Steps, adapted from Alcoholics Anonymous World Services, formed the basic structure from which the addicts were taught to reach out beyond themselves. The 'power' which could restore the addict to sanity, was acknowledged to be God. But this was an all-embracing view of God, a theosophical approach in which God was perceived through the individual's own understanding of him, rather than through the inspired word of God in the Bible, or the revealed Word become flesh we see in the person of Jesus. This, of course, explained Vicky's scepticism regarding the necessity of coming to Jesus as the only way to God. But at least with the new insight which our conversations had given me, I was enabled to pray more effectively, and with a fresh focus.

With the restoration of her faculties, however, Vicky became increasingly restless. Heroin had dominated her whole life for so long, filling the twenty-four hours of each day with the alternating urgency of securing the next fix, and the euphoria, bordering on oblivion, of having done so. Freed of the physical dependency, the days yawned empty and purposeless before her.

It was difficult, as her mother, to be completely objective. The emotional ties were too strong, and I was aware of the conflict stirring in my breast. How could I fail to rejoice in the fact that Vicky was free? Yet the uneasy feeling persisted. Free of what? Of the physical craving for heroin? But what of the psychological addiction?

Vicky had admitted to a 'needle addiction'. The idea was utterly abhorrent to me. I winced every time I thought of having to have an injection, but it had to be acknowledged that my revulsion did not in any way negate the reality of this phenomenon. It all comes back, I thought, to Satan's hold on the mind, whereby he seeks to woo us to a mentality of self-preoccupation and, ultimately, self-destruction. 'I suppose it's only a question of degree,' I remarked to Peter one day. 'Whether it's alcohol leading to drunkenness, slimming to anorexia, overeating to obesity, or whatever.'

Then, too, there were the root problems which had first caused Vicky to experiment with drugs. These, I was sure, were too deep-seated to be resolved only through counselling with Gerald or my little pep talks. Even prayer for healing could only be partial. Ultimately, I could see that nothing short of her complete submission to Jesus would restore her to wholeness.

With each passing day, Vicky's restlessness increased, so that in due course she approached me with a view to ascertaining whether my parents might have her to live with them. 'I'm not ready to go back to London,' she admitted, 'but I'm sorry, Mum, I just can't go on living

here.' Her face took on a pleading expression, begging
my unquestioning comprehension. 'You do understand,
don't you, Mum?'

I put it to my parents, telling them I would fully
understand if they felt unable to take on so demanding a
burden. No pressure was brought to bear, and I kept my
thoughts to myself. There was no need, in any case, for
them to be voiced, since I discovered that we were of one
mind. After a minimum of discussion between themselves, they agreed that Vicky would benefit from being
away from the sibling rivalry at home. Though they did
not say so, they may well have thought, as I did, that
Vicky also wanted to escape from the pressures of living
in a Christian home. 'Your father and I both feel she
needs to be king-pin for a while,' my mother said, 'and
with the best will in the world, that's not possible in your
home.'

And so, on a mellow day in early autumn, I took Vicky
to her new home. For the next few weeks my parents
went to town, deliberately setting out to spoil her, to
make her feel special, to demonstrate to her in every
way acceptable to her that she was loved and wanted.
New clothes began to appear on her back as my mother
allowed her to choose for herself, footing the bill at the
end. 'But I don't want her to feel bought,' she confided
to me, 'so we've agreed that after this, anything else is a
loan. I don't suppose Vicky will actually ever repay it,
but she seems to want it like that.'

They encouraged Vicky to find a little end-of-season
job, washing up in a local restaurant. It paid very little,
and was only part time, but it gave her some purpose in
life and brought her into contact with people living
ordinary, everyday lives. 'It means your father has to
collect her when she finishes late at night,' my mother
told me, 'she doesn't earn enough for a taxi, and we
wouldn't want her coming home alone in the dark, but
it's worth it to give her some feeling of self-worth.'

I hoped that my father wasn't wearing himself out,
but agreed that there was no alternative, living as they

did in the country some distance from the town. But there was no question of being over-indulgent. My mother seemed to get away with speaking to Vicky in a way which would have been totally unacceptable coming from me, standing no nonsense and really bossing her over her unkempt hair and dirty nails. Vicky seemed to thrive on it, almost welcoming the discipline which had so long been absent in her life. 'Perhaps a little more of that from her father and me in her childhood might have saved her from so much later,' I thought.

With the day-to-day tensions easing out of my own life, the Lord gave me two more scriptures, both of which I dated in my Bible, writing Vicky's name alongside. One spoke of sowing in tears and reaping in joy (Psalm 126:5), and as Vicky was persuaded by my parents to apply for a Government training opportunity scheme (TOPS), I wondered if this was to be the harvest. 'We've certainly done enough sowing in tears, Lord,' I thought. 'Will this training scheme be the opening of a whole new life for Vicky?'

15

A Baptism of Tears

'Meggie, your mother and I feel that some attempt should be made to trace Vicky.' My father faced me across the room, his kindly grey eyes showing concern beneath the head of fine silver hair. 'I'm quite prepared to contact the Salvation Army myself,' he continued, 'and will do so if you don't, but perhaps it would be better coming from you?'

Vicky had not gone ahead with the TOPS course, despite having secured a place after a six-week assessment course. After some months of living with my parents, she'd returned to London and for the past year had lived a drug-free life, moving from one squalid flat to another. Now, for the first time, we'd lost track of her altogether.

My parents had done so much for Vicky. How could I explain the Christian principles which I now felt applicable without hurting them further? Thanks for taking on my burden for Vicky, but I've decided now just to let her go since that seems to be what she wants? No! It would be kinder to them to trace her, whether or not that meant actually contacting her.

'I think I'll start by ringing all her old telephone numbers,' I explained to Peter that evening. 'Someone might know a forwarding address without my having to involve the Sally Army.'

Gathering up all the old letters I'd saved, plus my
address book, I sorted them into chronological order.
Then I spread them on the bed before me and began to
dial the London numbers, beginning with the most recent one. It rang and rang without reply. Working
backwards, I tried again. Some gave the same negative
result, others the unobtainable signal. Since many of
Vicky's previous abodes had been squats—properties
which were officially untenanted until taken over ille-
gally by the transient population of the city—I presumed that the landlords had had the line disconnected.
And who could blame them?

But that didn't help my cause. It was a frustrating
business listening endlessly to the futile ringing, but
eventually it seemed that my persistence paid off.

'Hello?' a foreign voice replied. Asian, I guessed, and
female.

'Could I please speak to Victoria Scott?' I began, relieved to have made some contact.

'Who that?' The disembodied voice sing-songed down
the phone.

Taking her enquiry to be with Vicky's name, rather
than mine, I repeated it, adding the diminutive several
times. 'Vicky. Vicky Scott.'

The line went dead.

Patiently, I redialled and less patiently waited for
some ten minutes while the phone kept ringing. Surely
someone would pick it up if only to silence it?

Discouraged, I gave up and tried another number,
making contact on this occasion with Vicky's employer
from her night-club days. We'd spoken previously when
she'd been working there—before I'd fully understood
the set-up—and I knew from Vicky that he was not only
au fait with her situation, but had shown considerable
sympathy and understanding.

'It's Vicky's mother here,' I said quickly, hoping to
avoid a repeat performance of being cut off. 'I wondered if you have any idea of her present whereabouts?'

I clutched the receiver tightly to my ear.

'Sorry. She left here over a year ago, probably nearer two.' The latest hit single playing loudly in the background all but obscured his reply.

'Yes, I know that. She's been living at home since then,' I continued hurriedly, anxious to establish that there was no real rift between us. 'It's just that I've lost her present address.'

Assuring me that he had not seen her for over a year, he was adamant in that he could give me no further information. I sighed. Extracting a promise from him to ask her to contact me should he see her in the future, I replaced the receiver. Somehow I doubted that he would tell me even if he had seen Vicky.

The Asian woman answered when I redialled the original number. 'This is Vicky Scott's mother, I began. 'I've lost her—'

'You have wrong number,' the other woman chimed in.

'Yes I know. I've lost contact with her. Can you tell me where she is?'

'I not know her.' The tone was emphatic.

'This is her mother,' I began to feel panicky, certain that this woman was lying. What was she trying to conceal? 'Are you a mother?' I asked her, aware that my voice was betraying my distress. 'Can you understand? She's my daughter. . . I've . . . I've lost her.'

'She not here. She not here for long time. She left long time ago.' There was considerable agitation in the voice, and before I could question her further, a scuffle ensued on the other end of the line.

'We not know your daughter. You understand?' A male voice barked down the phone.

'But your wife said she had left. You must have known her.'

'We not know her. She left here long time ago.'

Once again the line went dead.

I found the whole experience unnerving. There were so many inconsistencies. It was one thing to live in peace at home, lulled with Scripture verses, cut off from the reality of the situation. But contact with Vicky's way of life brought home the truth of just what she was into.

She could be dead. I might never know. Lying huddled in a doorway, without identification, who would bother to trace her to me? These people all seemed to stick together, united in their opposition to anything which smacked of morality, law and order, decency and respectability. Thick as thieves!

My father, who during his working life had had considerable experience of the seamier side of London life, had pointed out to me on one occasion when I'd threatened to 'shop' Patti, that to do so could be to endanger Vicky's life and possibly our own. 'These people stick together, but if one threatens their safety by divulging criminal activities to the police, you can be sure they would take retribution. Drugs are big business. Lives are expendable to those at the top.'

Remembering his words, I lost no time next morning in setting out a letter to the Salvation Army. After listing all previous known addresses, I found myself telling the whole story, beginning in Vicky's childhood, the problems at school, the divorce, the child psychiatrist who was of the opinion that I was a religious fanatic. The letter continued with mention of Vicky's intention of living with an alleged rapist, her thefts and court appearances, and the ensuing wardship proceedings. Details followed of the drunken brawl with her father, while she was on probation, and the three occasions when we had got her off the drugs. I continued:

Despite all this, I still love her and long to see her happy, living a wholesome life. Both her sisters are baptized believers and I believe that Vicky will need to come to the Lord before she will really be clear. However, I never push this at her—if she comes, it will be because he draws her. Vicky is now twenty-two years old. She has been landed in hospital on at least one occasion through overdosing, and has also had leg ulcers. She has virtually no veins left. I desperately need to know that she is safe, even if she doesn't want me to know where she is. I do hope that you can help. I am sorry to have written so much, I have tried to keep it as factual as possible, but find it difficult to control my own emotion.

Setting it all down on paper had proved a painful experience. The tears had been threatening throughout. Gathering force, they now burst forth as I sat at my desk. Weeping profusely, I sat transfixed, gulping for air as grief overcame me. It welled up from deep within, with a pain that was almost physical. I'd cried before, but this was something unfathomable, an anguish so deep it had never yet seen the light of day. It rose like a great tidal wave, sweeping everything before it, seeking liberty from the restraining forces of respectability and the pseudo-Christianity which denies the expression of emotion in the 'truly spiritually-minded'. It pounded on my senses with an energy which was exhausting, debilitating. It was unreasoning and unreasonable, blotting out all thought-processes in a mighty force of feeling.

And then at last it was spent, the silence and stillness an eerie contrast to all that had gone before. I sat at my desk, making no attempt to excuse or deny its having taken place, nor to analyse its meaning. All I knew was its purging and cleansing effect. And after the storm, there is peace.

The peace flooded through me, quietly, gently and calmly, like the incoming tide, filling the void within. Soothing and comforting, it transported me to another place, an ethereal world yet not unreal. This was reality, this was truth—this peace which was at once beyond yet within; this peace that is not of the world, perfect in tranquility, surpassing all human understanding.

I was reminded that evening, as I sat up in bed, of some of the verses the Lord had given me the previous year. They were Jeremiah 31:15–17. I'd dated them and put Vicky's name beside them in my Bible. Now, turning the pages by the mellow light of my bedside lamp, I read it anew:

This is what the Lord says: 'A voice is heard in Ramah, mourning and great weeping, Rachel weeping for her children and refusing to be comforted, because her children are no more.'

This is what the Lord says: 'Restrain your voice from weeping and your eyes from tears, for your work will be rewarded,' declares the Lord. 'They will return from the land of the enemy. So there is hope for your future,' declares the Lord, 'Your children will return to their own land.'

It was a whole year since the Lord had given me that promise. For twelve months and two days that covenant regarding Vicky had been mine. Yet could it be said that I'd derived blessing from it?

Only a few days ago, a week or two at most, I'd passed some remark, expressing my concern regarding Vicky, voicing doubt and despair as to her future.

'You know she's going to be the Lord's one day, Mummy,' Ruth had reminded me quietly. 'Have you forgotten how you saw her going down into the waters of baptism last year?'

Out of the mouths of babes . . . . I'd felt ashamed, yet proud, that Ruth whose faith was so tender and new had had to remind me of this truth.

'I have to live in the truth, live out the reality of that promise,' I said aloud in the empty bedroom. 'I have to restrain my voice from weeping, my eyes from tears. Faith is the hope of things unseen (Hebrews 11:1). Unless I hold fast to those things God has revealed to me, I am not exercising faith. I have to receive his promises. Only as I take hold of them—his most precious gifts to me—do they become mine, and only thus are they brought into being, to live, to have life and breath and substance. There is hope for the future. Vicky will return to her own land.'

As if to confirm this truth, the Lord showed me yet again that his arm is not too short. Within a few days, most probably at the prompting of one of the people to whom I'd spoken on the telephone, Vicky rang home.

She'd forgotten, she explained, just how long it was since last she'd been in touch!

Vicky again returned home for Christmas. It was obvious, as we all congregated for the duration of the festival at my parents' home, that she was enjoying better health than she had had for many years. Despite her incessant smoking and the resulting cough, her green eyes sparkled beneath a shining head of hair, now re-styled in such a way as to enhance her small oval face. A natural feminine vanity had spurred her into rubbing Vitamin E cream into her hands, arms and legs to rejuvenate the skin and alleviate the worst of the blackened scar-tissue.

Obviously enjoying the fact that she, of all the family, was most familiar with the new kitchen lay-out in my parent's home, she revelled in putting us all in our place, and adopted the role of daughter of the household. She spoke of various drug addict friends who had become Christians. Although she spoke mockingly of them, describing in detail their 'Bible-thumping, Jesus-oriented' lifestyle, I fancied it was not without affection mingled with a certain degree of admiration.

Still, I was not altogether at ease. Vicky had brought us all expensive presents, and Sarah had commented on the disparity between them when it came to financial standing. 'It seems to me that it's not worth working these days. You get more on the dole!'

'I just hope she's not mixed up with any credit-card racket,' her father remarked when phoning to speak to the girls. 'She was involved with a fellow a couple of years ago, you know, who worked some sort of fraudulent system.'

Short of confronting her, and risking a scene, there was no way of knowing. I knew Vicky's response would be one of outrage. 'Don't you trust me?' she would demand. It had to be left to the Lord. He'd proved over and over again that nothing was beyond him, and that he not only knew her through and through, but that she was far too precious to him to abandon her in any way.

'It's quite incredible that she's still alive,' said one well-meaning friend as I related the story to her one evening when she was visiting our church. It's more than incredible, I thought, it's a miracle.

But when Vicky paid a flying visit home for my birthday, some months after Christmas, it was very evident from her restless behaviour that all was not as it should be. And after her return to London, this conviction grew.

'I feel that the Lord is prompting me to write to her—just to let her know that I love her,' I confided to a friend who was also my prayer partner. 'I think she might be in trouble again and needs to know that I won't cut her off.' My friend had felt similarly while praying for Vicky, and together we committed to the Lord a brief letter opening the way to further communication.

The result was instantaneous. Vicky rang within days.

'I'm sorry I haven't been in touch, Mum. I haven't been very well recently.'

'Oh? Is it this flu that's going around?' I enquired.

'No.' There was silence, then, as if choosing her words carefully, 'I've got a bad hand.'

'A bad hand?' I furrowed my brow. 'What have you done?'

'I'm in hospital, Mum.'

'In hospital?' Peter, passing beside me where I sat on the bottom stair, turned his head enquiringly as I repeated Vicky's words. 'Don't know,' I mouthed, shrugging my shoulders and spreading my free hand palm up.

'Yes, Mum,' Vicky paused expectantly.

'Whatever's the matter?' Deliberately, I made no assumptions.

'Oh, Mum!' I closed my eyes and shot an arrow prayer to the Lord as understanding began to dawn on me. 'I hit an artery,' she explained reluctantly. 'My hand just ballooned in seconds. I've had to have injections into my stomach every few hours ever since to reduce the swelling.'

It was difficult to know what to say. Briefly I shut my eyes again, blotting out the familiar sights of furnishings, ornaments and pictures on the wall. In my mind's eye I visualized Vicky, alone in the bleak surroundings of a London hospital. Would she never learn? It was disappointing news—and yet I knew peace. It was strange really, but there was no anxiety. The peace that had spread through me remained, giving me a new serenity. Of course, Vicky's graphic details made me feel squeamish, yet inwardly I knew that my reaction, humanly speaking, was most unnatural.

'It's almost as if the Lord will not let Vicky be free of her addiction until she turns to him.' I explained to Peter as I replaced the receiver and returned to the lounge. 'My prayer was that she would never know peace or comfort in the way of life she's chosen. That's precisely what's happening. I'm becoming increasingly convinced that Vicky's freedom is conditional. The Lord's going to be the only way out for her.'

'She's certainly had some narrow escapes, humanly speaking,' he replied, laying aside his newspaper. 'There's no doubt that the Lord has kept her through all this. Anyone else would have died long ago.' I had to agree. It really was incredible.

She was like a fish, caught in a net, struggling wildly in an effort to escape, to return to the environment from whence she came. If only she would be still long enough to understand that the net spelled life—freedom and life.

'What do you want to do about her?' Peter regarded me thoughtfully across the room, his long legs stretched before him in an attitude of relaxation. When it came to decisions about the girls, he felt he should not interfere but offer counsel only when asked. If I wanted Vicky home again, I knew I had only to say so. He would never stand between me and my daughters.

But that wasn't the answer. Of that I was sure. Since the writing of my letter to the Salvation Army, and the experience which had followed, the Lord had been speaking to me in many ways.

'I don't think we should offer to help her off the drugs at home again, do you?' I looked enquiringly at Peter for confirmation, and taking his slow nod to be a sign of approval, went on, 'I think I'll give her Eric Blakebrough's telephone number.'

We'd heard him speaking locally only a week or two ago, and had been most impressed with the work which the Lord had so obviously begun twenty years previously when Kaleidoscope had been set up in the Bunyan Baptist Church. Its aim then, as now, was to demonstrate in as complete a way as possible what the kingdom of God means in practice. Among the many ways in which these aims are achieved is the reaching out to drug addicts with loving, caring, professional help and rehabilitation.

'I've come more and more to the conclusion,' I continued, 'that Vicky will never come to the Lord through us. There are too many reminders here of a past that smacks of religious hyprocrisy to her.' I put my head on one side, new thoughts forming in my mind even as I spoke. 'If we're right in believing that she'll never be free of the drugs until she accepts the Lord, then I'm convinced it's going to have to be through someone else.'

Peter nodded, pulling himself upright in his chair and leaning forwards, arms resting on his knees. 'Yes, I think you're right. But I don't think the times she's been home have been wasted.'

'How do you mean?' I leaned back, resting my head in my hand.

'Well, there's no question of Vicky feeling that we can't be bothered with her,' he explained.

'That's true.' Encouraged, I pulled myself upright. 'It's good to see how the Lord has used what could so easily be seen as a waste of time and effort. Vicky must realize that she's loved, and it's certainly opened up communication between herself and the family. There was a time when I thought she'd walked out for good, after the wardship business.'

'Mmm.' Peter stood up, extending a hand to help me from my chair. 'It's been a bridge-building experience,' he smiled as together we went up to bed.

Vicky rang again over the next few days, and I was able to put her in touch with Kaleidoscope. There seemed to be an unspoken understanding between us that though we were not in any way shunning her, and that home was an open door any time she wanted to visit, there was no longer any question of our being able to help her come off the drugs.

A subsequent conversation with the staff confirmed for me that Vicky did indeed make contact while she was still in the hospital, though it later transpired that she never followed this through. Once again, as the months rolled by, we lost contact, though I was led to understand by her flatmates that she was back with her prostitute friend.

'I had a strange dream last night,' I said to Peter when we woke earlier than usual one Saturday morning. 'I saw Jesus stretching out his hand to Mary Magdalene. That was all. But even in my sleep I knew that the Lord was speaking to me of Vicky. "I am there, even in that situation" he said gently. "Even there, she is not beyond my reach." He was so loving and gentle, it made me cry.' Propped up on my pillows, as the dawn crept through the curtains, I marvelled at the steadfastness of our God.

16

On the Water's Edge

What have I learned? Sitting at my desk once more, I stared contemplatively at the wall before me. Several months had elapsed since Vicky's last visit home, months in which to draw together the strands of truth and trial, fact and faith. They'd been, during the event, a haphazard conglomerate of mixed emotions; trust intertwined with fear, grief with gladness, and revulsion mingled with compassion. Interwoven by the passage of time, they'd become the fabric by which to answer the queries I'd set myself at the onset of this quest for knowledge. A unique but recognizable pattern had emerged.

'You know what I think your next book should be,' our pastor had said to me sometime ago. 'You ought to share with others what the Lord's brought you through with Vicky.' I'd fought shy of this suggestion for a while, feeling it would somehow be a breach of loyalty to Vicky and many others to put the story into print. 'And what do I have to share?' I'd asked myself. 'There's no happy ending.' But now I know otherwise. With God there is always a happy ending. 'It's just that the story isn't yet ended,' I smiled at Peter, as we walked down to the seafront later in the evening. 'But we have learned lessons along the way, haven't we?'

A palid moon hung limply in the purple hue of dusk,

its faint radiance outshone by the garlands of brightly coloured lights, dipping gracefully from lamp post to lamp post along the promenade. The gentle lapping of tiny waves, as they licked against the concrete steps, was a tiny whisper, barely discernible above the roar of the traffic. Yet the borrowed light reflected from the silvery disc proceeded from a power billions of times greater than the few thousand sixty-watt bulbs strung along the seafront. And the docile ocean was a tamed and harnessed energy of infinite force and strength, far surpassing that created by man. Thus, in the clamouring voices of this world, is the still small voice of God.

'It was right to do what we did,' I said as we stood beneath the sea-wall. 'That day last summer, when Vicky and I had our altercation in her bedroom—when I asked her forgiveness—it had to be done, though my father mightn't agree. He says that Freud produced a generation of 'guilty' parents, and that consequently we live in a society which absolves people from responsibility for their own actions. We blame everyone but the culprit.'

'Do you disagree with that?' Peter led me to a bench where we could sit and watch the lights sparkling off the water.

'Oh no.' I smoothed my skirt beneath me. 'I think he's right. John White says in his book *Parents in Pain* (IVP) that when a parent has done all he can do for the good of the child, that child still has free will to do as he chooses. We shouldn't take on guilt and condemnation if they make bad choices.' I scooped up a handful of pebbles and threw them one by one into the water before continuing. 'But nevertheless, we are imperfect, and I believe that it's only when we confess our fault and ask forgiveness that the power of God is released to work in the lives of our children. After all, it was only when I'd begged Vicky's forgiveness for my bad parenting that she was released to admit her own guilt and responsibility.'

'So what you're saying is that a drug addict is as he is

because he chooses to be?' Peter raised an eyebrow.

I paused for a moment, intent on a small group of ducks swimming towards us out of the twilight. 'Yes and no,' I replied, a faint frown creasing my brow. 'We all have free will, but do we really understand what we're choosing? If a person really understood the horror of his potential bondage to drugs, his absolute inability ever to be free again, and the hell he would live through before reaching a premature death, do you think he would go ahead? I believe it's because Satan comes like a wolf in sheep's clothing—an angel of light—that people are taken in,' I went on. 'Just as a child molester offers sweeties to tempt his victim, so the Enemy whispers promises of a counterfeit heaven: "Take this tiny quantity of heroin and you will be transported to paradise, to heavenly raptures where all the pain and problems of this world will fade into oblivion."' I shivered involuntarily and made to stand up. 'What he doesn't tell you about' I concluded, 'is the living hell that comes later.'

I drew my jacket around me as we turned homewards. C.S. Lewis, I remembered, had described hell as a 'place never made for men at all' and that those who enter that place are not men but the 'remains' of a humanity consisting of 'a will utterly centred in its self and passions utterly uncontrolled by the will' (*The Problem of Pain* (Fontana/Collins), p.101). What more apt description could there be for those whose addiction leads them into a hell on earth? The addict is only the 'remains', living in a place not meant for humanity.

The grass beneath our feet was damp with dew as we walked back across the meadows. Here and there the fruits of an ancient mulberry tree, mingling with the sparkling droplets, ran red as blood. Vicky had been bought and paid for by the blood of Jesus. In cutting her off from the influence and oppression of the Enemy, we'd set her free to choose Christ, to choose salvation, to choose life. With the bonds cut, her hands were at liberty to accept God's gift. But even he would not force her choice. To do so would revoke the freedom he'd endowed upon us all.

'One thing I have come to realize,' I squeezed Peter's hand as we strolled back through the park, dwarfed on all sides by towering conifers.

'And what's that?' He smiled down at me, well used to my sudden outbursts after periods of silent meditation.

'I know that whatever we see with our eyes is not re-ality unless we see also with the eyes of the Spirit. The circumstances around us are only shadows. Real truth lies in seeing God's hand in the situation. And whether it works out to our satisfaction or not, God is still to be trusted. Our ideas of a satisfactory solution to the prob-lems of life are a totally inadequate yardstick by which to measure his greatness. We can't judge the Judge.'

Before us the massive ironwork of the park gates, illumined now only by the street lamps, traced a delicate fretwork against the darkening sky. Hurrying a little as a cool breeze blew up, I continued breathlessly to expound my thoughts. 'Neither can we judge the right or wrong of our actions by the results we see. Whether Vicky stays off the drugs or not, I believe it was right to help her. Jesus was far more discerning than we are, but he never turned anyone away—even those who didn't accept what he had to offer. And he must have known who they were beforehand.'

Peter tucked my hand through his arm to see me across the road. A man of few words, he had proved nevertheless to be a tremendous source of strength and wisdom in my life. There was a rapport between us which needed no verbal affirmation. I knew that if he felt I was wrong in my assessment of the situation, he would soon tell me. And he knew that I knew.

As the road took an upward turn, making it too steep for easy conversation, I fell once more into silence. Vicky's salvation doesn't depend on my desire or effort, I thought, but on God's mercy. His word says: 'I will have mercy on whom I have mercy, and I will have compassion on whom I have compassion' (Romans 9:15). I can do no more for her than love her. And my love, like his, must be unconditional, accepting her as she is, whether or not she changes. Throughout her life, wherever her free will has taken her, the Lord has proved that there is *nothing* that is not subject to him. 'What is man that you are mindful of him, the son of man that you care for him? You made him a little lower than the angels; you crowned him with glory and honour and put everything under his feet' (Hebrews 2:7–8).

Panting slightly as we reached the top of the hill, we turned to look back at the evening sky. Only a faint luminosity lingered on the horizon, defining the divide of sky and sea. Far to the right, perched on a massive cliff-head starkly silhouetted against the gathering gloom, a tiny speck of light shone momentarily and was gone, then it came again, and was gone. 'Ten seconds between flashes, then thirty,' Peter explained, his arm around my shoulders. 'All lighthouses have a different sequence.'

To me this tiny pin-prick of light in a dark sea, is symbolic. I have peace. I have come to accept that Vicky may not surrender to the Lord until, like the thief on the cross, she does so with her dying breath. But though I grieve for the waste of her young life, I know that God's promises are to be trusted.

The vision of the net and the water's edge was a prophecy of the future. Though God will not violate Vicky's free will, he knows the end from the beginning. And he has chosen to reveal it to me. Who can doubt that vision coming to fruition? 'Not one of all the Lord's good promises to the house of Israel failed; every one was fulfilled' (Joshua 21:45). That same Lord has fulfilled two thirds of my vision in bringing Sarah and Ruth into the fold. He will surely not fail on the final part.

My daughter has paddled in the waters of life. She is in the net of the Lord. And ultimately she will stand in the palm of his hand.

Appendix

Useful addresses

Blenheim Project, 7 Thorpe Close, London W10.
Tel. (01) 960 5599.
Families Anonymous, 88 Caledonian Road,
London N1 9DN. Tel. (01) 278 8805.
Kaleidoscope Project, 40–46 Cromwell Road,
Kingston-upon-Thames, Surrey. Tel. (01) 549 2681.
Lifeline Project, Jodrell Street, Manchester M3 3HE.
Tel. (061) 832 6353. (Write or phone for Christian
advice and a directory of drug facilities.)
Narcotics Anonymous, P.O. Box 246, London SW10.
Tel. (01) 871 0505.
SCODA (Standing Conference on Drug Abuse), 3
Blackburn Road, London NW6 1XA. Tel. (01) 328
6556.

Children at Risk

by David Porter

Our children—precious, inquisitive, vulnerable

This is an exciting age for children, where whole worlds of fantasy games, books and computers can be explored. Cinema and television excel in spectacular entertainment and stimulating education.

But there are risks.

David Porter, author and parent, takes us through some of the products and influences that are winning the minds of our children. While welcoming the wealth of creativity that so many bring, he sounds important warning notes for all those who wish to protect children from the nastier and more sinister elements of the market place. Finally we are alerted to the increasing physical danger our children face, as David looks at the unspoken risk of sexual abuse and the sale of drugs to under-fifteen-year-olds.

Parents and teachers will find this book a mine of information as well as a stirring manifesto for action. Brilliantly researched yet easy to read, it steers a course between the twin extremes of ill-advised panic and foolish complacency, showing us where the dangers lie and where we can tread the ground more confidently.

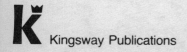

Kingsway Publications